THE LOAF THAT BECAME A LEGEND

A HISTORY OF SAINT JOHN'S BREAD

The Loaf That Became a Legend

A History of Saint John's Bread

Kenneth M. Jones
Diane Veale Jones

NORTH STAR PRESS OF ST. CLOUD, INC.

Printed in the United States of America by Versa Press, Inc., East Peoria, Illinois.

Published by: North Star Press of St. Cloud, Inc.
              P.O. Box 451
              St. Cloud, Minnesota 56302

Acknowledgments

This work was greatly enriched by the many people who shared their memories of some part of the story.

Isabelle and George Durenberger, Abbot Baldwin Dworschak, OSB, Peggy Gagliardi, Lee Hanley, Fred Hughes, Tom Juettner, Father Florian Muggli, OSB, Father Gervase Soukup, OSB, Father Francis Studer, OSB, Dr. Betty Sullivan, and Father Vincent Tegeder, OSB, all provided insights into Saint John's, the bread program, and Father Walter Reger, OSB.

Tom LeNeau, Jerry Mead, and Father Gordon Tavis, OSB, were invaluable for understanding events after Father Walter's death, while Norm Groth and Ray Thelen provided perspective on the baking industry. Rich Ruprecht contributed great stories about being the Johnnie Bread baker.

The Sisters of Saint Francis of the Immaculate Heart of Mary, Hankinson, North Dakota, provided us with hospitality, as well as Sister M. Patricia Forest's history *Prairie Praise* and Sister Gertrude (Witrada) Sperr's memories of working at Collegeville in the 1930s.

Ken would also like to thank all those who helped with the tedious task of transcribing the interviews. Brenda Levinski and Rachel Green did the bulk of the work with patience, accuracy, and good humor. Rob Buffington helped translate letters relating to the Mexican Benedictines.

Finally, a special thanks to Father Vincent Tegeder because, without him, this book would not have been written. It was his idea that started us and his encouragement that sustained us.

Dedicated to:

Father Vincent Tegeder, OSB

Table of Contents

THE LOAF THAT BECAME A LEGEND

A HISTORY OF SAINT JOHN'S BREAD

The Twin Towers of the old abbey church served as a symbol of Saint John's for decades and dominated the Collegeville landscape until they were removed in 1960. As this photograph reveals, the abbey and university were concentrated in the Quadrangle in 1886, and the "Devil's Tower" staircase on the northwest corner had not yet been added. (Photo courtesy of Saint John's Abbey Archives, Collegeville, Minnesota)

Chapter One

In the Beginning

In 1858, Brother Wolfgang Beck stood alone in a crude log house on what would become the Collegeville farm when "the door was softly opened and in stepped an Indian" who indicated that he wanted something to drink. Sharing the commonly held stereotypes about his New World neighbor, Brother Wolfgang assumed that the Indian wanted whiskey. Since he had none, the frightened monk shook his head and pointed to a pail of water in the room. With some relief, Brother Wolfgang reported that "the Indian seemed to understand the invitation and quietly left after the Brother had given him half a loaf of bread."[1]

As anyone who has visited Saint John's Abbey knows, the tradition of sharing bread with visitors has continued as a staple of Benedictine hospitality. Over the years, the bread baked in the abbey/university kitchens has delighted thousands of monks, students, and guests with its unique flavor and texture. "Johnnie Bread," as it came to be called, thus established itself as much a part of the Saint John's tradition as the Twin Towers, the Breuer Bell Banner, and famous coaches. But where did this delight come from, and how did the legend evolve?

When the men who would ultimately found Saint John's Abbey left Metten in Bavaria in the 1840s, they took their faith, a desire to serve their countrymen in the New World, and a treasured "*Schwarzbrot*" or black bread that formed a central part of their diet. While no recipe for the original *Schwarzbrot* has survived, it was most likely composed largely of rye flour, which would have produced a loaf that was dark, relatively flat, and quite dense. The monks' attachment to this familiar staple was rooted in economics and agricultural history.

1

Throughout the Middle Ages and well into the modern period, most people in what is now southern Germany ate dark breads composed of the easily grown rye and barley flours. While dark bread was the norm, "white" bread made from wheat flour was preferred because its color made it much easier to detect dirt and other impurities.[2] The masses, however, had little access to the lighter breads, for most wheat flour was imported and significantly more expensive.[3] Consumption of white bread was, therefore, a sign of status and confined primarily to the upper class.[4] This situation did not change significantly until after the first Benedictines had left Metten for the United States.[5]

Given this background, it seems quite likely that a later characterization of the very early bread of the Benedictines as "a black bread with about the density of pumpernickel" seems appropriate.[6] By immigrating to the United States, however, the monks found themselves in a setting where wheat for the higher-status white bread was readily available. As a result, consumption patterns probably began to change as soon as Abbot Boniface Wimmer and the first contingent of German Benedictines arrived at St. Vincent's Archabbey in Pennsylvania in 1846. As one historian of St. Vincent's notes, although rye was grown, wheat quickly became the primary grain cultivated. Furthermore, when the monks of the archabbey built a gristmill in 1854, they immediately installed a sifting bolt.[7] This enabled them to produce a rough equivalent of today's unbleached white flour rather than settling for the whole wheat that came directly off the milling stones.[8] They could, therefore, make something that twentieth-century consumers would recognize as a white bread. To this day, Saint Vincent's produces both a white and a whole wheat bread from grain ground at its mill.[9]

The Benedictines who settled in Minnesota followed a similar but slightly different path. With Stearns County farmers growing eight times as much wheat as rye as early as 1862, the preferred flour was easily available.[10] The monks took advantage of this, purchasing twenty to thirty times as much wheat per year as rye in the 1870s.[11] While the imbalance may have been rectified somewhat by rye grown on the 170 or so acres of cultivated abbey land, it is clear that less than two decades after their arrival in Minnesota, the monks were eating a lot of predominantly wheat-based white bread.[12] At the same time, however, the traditional rye-based *Schwarzbrot* didn't disappear from their diet immediately. According to one recollection of Saint John's at the turn of the century, monks frequently combined "a thick slice of black bread and a slice of white, sandwich style, to eat with coffee."[13]

2

The First Johnnie Bread

The bread that the Collegeville community of the late nineteenth century termed white was the true precursor of today's Johnnie Bread, although it was probably somewhat coarser and darker than the current version. One key to the difference lies in the milling techniques available. When the Benedictines were establishing the abbey at its current site in the 1860s, there were two gristmills in Saint Joseph, owned respectively by Ferdinand Danzl and John Henry Linnemann.[14] Both were relatively primitive processes that pulverized the entire wheat berry in one step, thus producing a flour that included bran and wheat germ as well.

In 1874, the monks erected their own mill on the banks of Watab Creek.[15] A somewhat more sophisticated apparatus with three runs of grinding stones, this mill would have been able to strip much of the bran on the first grinding, leaving a purer flour.[16] At the same time, however, there is no evidence of a sifter, so the flour produced at Collegeville was undoubtedly richly textured and a far cry from the finely ground, uniform flour of today. Indeed, even while they were doing their own milling, the monks purchased the finer flour for communion wafers from the commercial mills of the Twin Cities.[17]

After the Watab Creek mill was destroyed by fire in 1882, the abbey used Linnemann's new steam-powered mill in Saint Joseph. Since this was also a three-run mill, the wheat flour

The first Saint John's flour mill (on the right) was erected on the east side of Watab Creek in 1874. The new sawmill (on the left) replaced one that had burned in 1873. The new sawmill and flour mill served the community until they were both destroyed by fire on December 16, 1882. Father Alexius Hoffmann, OSB, commented that arson was suspected but "not plausible." (Photo courtesy of Saint John's Abbey Archives)

it produced was consistent with what the monks had ground themselves, even though it had a sifter to produce unbleached white flour. Local commercial mills evidently sufficed until 1918, when the abbey constructed a new building to house an electrically powered American Midget Marvel Flour Mill.[18] The reasons for doing so are lost, but the monks may have been drawn by the Midget Marvel's claims that it was so clean that one had been sold to the famous Kellogg Food Company of Battle Creek, Michigan.[19] They also may have been attracted by the profit potential, for the new mill required only one person for operation but could produce a lot more flour than needed by the abbey and university. Although Father Alexius Hoffmann wrote that it "grinds only for home use," financial records for the early 1920s show that the mill produced a slight profit by milling grain for local farmers.[20] By the early 1950s, however, the abbey no longer found it economical to mill its own flour, and the building was in such poor condition that demolition was recommended.[21] Eventually, in 1958, the mill was torn down to make way for Saint Thomas Aquinas Hall.[22]

Although improvements in local milling facilities would have permitted Saint John's to shift to a more refined white bread, the monks refused to follow the lead of most of the nation. Instead, they continued to prefer the loaf that would become a legend—a bread whose basic ingredients and texture were

This brick building, nestled among abbey farm buildings, housed the second flour mill. Students rejoiced at its construction because it meant that "there need be no fear that we shall run short of white or black bread this winter." In the mid-1920s, when this photo was taken, the mill not only provided flour for Saint John's bread but also did some milling for local farmers. The mill eventually fell into disuse and was torn down in 1958 to make way for Saint Thomas Aquinas Hall. (Photo courtesy of Saint John's Abbey Archives)

4

This electric American Midget Marvel Flour Mill was installed in the second flour mill when it was built in 1918. The machine was advertised as being so clean that it was used by the health and sanitation conscious Kellogg Food Company of Battle Creek, Michigan. Someone at Saint John's must have been worried about upholding that sanitary tradition: note the sign on the mill that reads, "Don't Spit On The Floor." (Photo courtesy of Saint John's Abbey Archives)

shaped by conditions in central Minnesota in the late nineteenth century. Johnnie Bread was distinct not only because of the mixture of one part rye flour to four parts wheat, but because the wheat portion included some relatively unpulverized bits that were very hard and could create a real surprise for the unwary eater.[23]

As milling techniques produced more uniform flour, the bakers at Saint John's added cracked wheat and cracked rye to maintain the nineteenth-century texture. In addition to its sometimes crunchy interior, older alumni also remember Johnnie Bread as having a distinctively crisp crust. This indicates that the original recipe used water rather than milk, which would soften the texture of both the bread and the crust. For the same reason, the original bread probably didn't include lard; this was added sometime before the 1940s, enhancing the flavor and the bread's keeping quality.[24] Finally, the recipe probably contained a little sugar, most likely in the form of honey, which would have speeded the fermentation of the yeast and contributed to a darker crust.

Brother William Baldus

Brother William Baldus, OSB, the monastery's chief cook for more than two decades after his entry into the order in 1869, formulated the loaf that would become a legend. While monks and students praised him as a creative chef, local children knew him as a soft touch for cookies and other treats. (Photo courtesy of Saint John's Abbey Archives)

The originator of this new wheat-based dark bread was most probably Brother William Baldus, the new community's third cook.[25] Brother William was born in Germany in 1844, served in the German army during the war of 1866 and then came to the United States in 1868. After a brief stint in the kitchens at the Ryan Hotel in Saint Paul, Brother William joined the Collegeville community and took over the cook's duties soon after he entered the novitiate in 1869.[26] A very creative and well-loved chef, Brother William earned praise from both students and alumni for the "sumptuous feasts" he prepared. He was renown for his cranberry pie but was also particularly adept at preparing wild game shot in the woods.[27] Skilled and inventive, Brother William no doubt responded to the community's changing tastes and the availability of relatively cheap wheat flour in the New World by formulating what would become known as Johnnie Bread.

Brother William baked his bread in an open hearth oven built entirely of brick. A student just after the turn of the century recalled it as "a brick beehive-shaped unit about eight feet high and five feet wide. Cordwood sticks were fed into the lower section, with the flames heating up a heavy sheet of iron on which the bread was placed."[28] The loaves, which were about eighteen inches long and eight inches wide, were typically cut into slices about five-eighths of an inch thick before being placed on the table. Brother William used a specially constructed two-foot-long knife for this process.[29]

By the 1890s, Brother William's health made it difficult for him to continue to run the kitchen. He served briefly at Saint Peter's Abbey in Saskatchewan and spent a year at Saint Martin's in Washington, hoping the change in climate would ease his rheumatism. While in Collegeville, Brother William worked intermittently as chief cook until his official retirement in 1904.[30] During this period, the kitchen was increasingly staffed by male laymen, including John Powers, who was listed as the chief cook in 1896-1897. This evidently did not work too well, for there was a very high rate of turnover.[31] Finally, the "continued difficulty of procuring suitable male hands to conduct the kitchen" caused

By the 1890s, the abbey was no longer able to find sufficient kitchen staff among its members, so increasing numbers of local laymen and boys were hired. These unidentified kitchen workers were photographed in the middle of the decade and may include John Powers, who was the first non-Benedictine to hold the position of chief cook. (Photo courtesy of Saint John's Abbey Archives)

the abbey to break tradition and invite women into the male preserve.[32] Thirteen French Sisters of the Presentation arrived in May 1904, taking up temporary residence in the Carpentry Shop until more suitable quarters were erected.[33] When the sisters took charge, the monks were told that "henceforth breakfast would not be served until 6:00 A.M., and that we are to rise at 4:00 A.M. instead of 3:45," but apparently little changed in terms of the food served.[34] Despite their hard work, it was soon clear that the

When the French Sisters of the Presentation arrived in Collegeville, this building was constructed to house them. Only a few yards from the kitchens, it was successively occupied by the French, German and Mexican nuns who cooked for the students and monks at Saint John's. After the last group of nuns departed, the building became a fairly infamous party dorm known as Frank House, but it has since been reconsecrated as the Saint John's Seminary. (Photo courtesy of Saint John's Abbey Archives)

thirteen sisters couldn't meet the needs of the approximately one hundred monks and four hundred students at Collegeville. Evidently unable to recruit more domestic help from what was generally a teaching order, Abbot Peter Engel began to search for more assistance from a different source. He was ultimately successful when he approached Mother General Innocentia Mussak of the Franciscans of Dillingen, Bavaria, in 1913.[35]

Recruiting the Franciscans, or the "German sisters" as they became known, meant a relatively permanent solution to the problem of finding quality kitchen staff. Not only did the Franciscans have a tradition of domestic service, but a growing convent and Mother General Innocentia's commitment to missionary work spurred her to meet the abbot's request for twenty-four nuns. Although World War I temporarily disrupted the flow, Dillingen continued to supply the abbey's needs during the interwar years, as over one hundred more Franciscans came to the New World, with most working for at least a while at Saint John's.[36] Since they shared a south German heritage with many of the monks of the abbey, adjustments in language, culture, and food habits were minimized. Even the more Americanized stu-

The Franciscan nuns were known by students and monks alike as the "German Sisters"; they were generally Bavarian born, spoke German, and wore their distinctive Dillingen veil (pictured) until after World War II. When this photo was taken in 1934, Sister Angeline Altoff (ninth from the right in the third row) was the only non-German among the sisters at Saint John's. Sister Angeline, born in Adrian, Minnesota, professed in 1931 and was one of three teachers at the local elementary school who were included in this photo. Four visiting sisters are pictured; the other thirty-three worked in the kitchens. Mother Superior Paschalina Schaflitzel is seated in the center front. Sister Joffrieda Kolnsperger (second from left in first row) arrived at Saint John's with the first group of Franciscans in 1913 and stayed until they left in 1958. Sister Jordana Mayer (far right in first row) was also among the last four Franciscans at Collegeville. While many of the nuns stayed for years, not all were content. One who came in 1922 was happy to move to Hankinson, North Dakota, in 1928 when the Franciscans began their motherhouse there. Admitting that "I couldn't stand that bread [at Saint John's]," one of her first actions in Hankinson was to purchase some white store bread. (Photo courtesy of the Archives of the Sisters of Saint Francis, Hankinson, North Dakota)

dents quickly came to praise the new help, for as the campus newspaper, the *Record*, noted in 1913, "Though unused to American customs, the Sisters soon served up dishes in the most approved American style. Under their able hands, the fame of 'Black Bread' has not diminished a whit."[37]

For forty-five years, from 1913 until 1958, the Franciscan sisters served those who lived in Collegeville. One, Sister Joffrieda Kolnsperger, worked in the kitchens for the whole period. Another of the stalwarts was Sister Witrada (Gertrude) Sperr, who arrived at Collegeville from Dillingen in 1938. In charge of the dining room for most of the period, Sister Gertrude arose at 5:00 A.M. every day, helped with all three meals, and fell into bed at 9:00 P.M. The rest of the daily routine included mass in the morning, office in the afternoon, and a brief recreation period before bed. In her spare time, she darned socks for the seminarians. Still, as Sister Gertrude recalled, the monks "took nice care for us" by providing two masses a day in the nuns' chapel so that work schedules didn't deprive them of their daily communion.[38]

Despite their dedication, the work gradually overwhelmed the sisters. To a large extent, this was caused by the growth of the school, for, by 1952 the sisters reported that "we cook three times a day for 1,340 people."[39] At the same time, the creation of a new motherhouse in Hankinson, North Dakota, and the emergence of new apostolates meant that few Franciscans were available for kitchen duty. Increasingly, the abbey used the nuns to supervise a growing cadre of student and lay workers.

In remodeled kitchens and a new veil, the Franciscan sisters continued to serve at Saint John's after World War II. In the center, Sister Irene is stacking Johnnie Bread on a tray of plates held by Sister Gerelinde. A Saint John's *Record* writer described the Franciscans as "sparkling, gracious nuns who work while we study, while we play, while we sleep, and even while we eat," and urged his fellow Johnnies to "give a thought to our good sisters who spend hours preparing what we consume in minutes." (Photo from the *Record*, December 19, 1946, and courtesy of Saint John's University Archives)

Arriving from Dillingen in 1938, Sister Gertrude (Witrada) Sperr was one of the last of the Bavarian-born sisters to come to Saint John's. In charge of the dining room, she stayed until the last of the Franciscans left for the provincial motherhouse in Hankinson, North Dakota. Under her watchful eye, the nuns (and later local girls who worked as servers) set and cleared the tables, making sure that there were large stacks of fresh-baked Johnnie Bread available at every meal. Even though her day began at 5:00 A.M. and she darned socks for seminarians in her spare time, Sister Gertrude still had fond memories of her years in Collegeville when this photo was taken in 1995. (Photo by Ken Jones)

Ultimately, however, the Franciscans decided that they had to give up the effort. In 1958, the last four—Sisters Joffrieda, Witrada, Jordana Mayer, and Bernadette Jaeger—left Collegeville for Hankinson.

As it became increasingly apparent that the Franciscans' long service was coming to an end, the abbey once again looked outside for women whose religious devotion made them willing to serve as kitchen help for the monks and students. Working through Prior Clarus Graves, who previously had been the prior of the Saint John's Foundation at Colegio del Tepeyac in Mexico City, Abbot Baldwin turned to the Benedictines of Cristo Rey de Guadalupe, asking them to supply nuns "to be used here for work in the kitchen and refectory, as well as for making and repairing of religious habits of our community."[40]

Although Abbot Baldwin began his efforts to recruit Mexican sisters in 1955, the first four didn't arrive until 1958. At that point, after a short period of tutelage under the remaining Franciscans, the Mexican Benedictines took over the kitchens and the production of the essential Johnnie Bread.[41] By 1959, twenty of the new sisters had settled in Collegeville, but, for several reasons, their numbers quickly began to shrink.[42] By 1962, there were only thirteen left, and Prior Clarus was begging Mother Superior M. Placida Barrios for more. The prior promised that the nuns were happier now since they were able to work together, but that this arrangement was threatened by the dwindling numbers. If more weren't sent soon, those in Collegeville would have to interact more with lay people, which the abbot didn't think proper.[43] Despite the prior's entreaties and the mother superior's efforts, the Mexican connection soon failed. By 1964, the baking of Johnnie Bread had been permanently turned over to lay employees.

Bread at Every Meal

No matter who made the bread, it played a central role in the diet of the monks and students at Saint John's. In the early years, following the German pattern, four or five meals were served each day with bread either as the sole item or as a central part of the meal. As Father Alexius Edelbrock, one of the first students and later the second abbot, recalled:

> We had to rise at five o'clock, say our morning prayers, attend daily Mass, then study and seven o'clock breakfast: i.e. a cup of coffee—if such it could be called—and a slice of dry bread, no butter or molasses or sugar there. . . . At dinner a

watery black soup with plenty of bread in it invariably made its appearance. . . . After soup came potatoes and meat—never more than one kind—then bread. . . . At three o'clock, we received a piece of dry bread. This, with fresh water, was relished with gusto . . . at six o'clock supper the first dish was again the indispensable soup, the rest usually as at noon.[44]

Once the abbey moved from Saint Cloud to Collegeville and became more established, meals became a little less spartan and more varied. While it is not possible to reconstruct the daily diet, account books do offer some insight. In 1874-1875, the abbey purchased $1,211.95 in undifferentiated "victuals" from McQuilland and Company. Another $2,348 was spent on itemized entries in the same category. The primary purchases were butter, beef, wheat, and potatoes, but there were less frequent expenditures for pigs, sheep, chickens, venison, geese, and cranberries.[45] (A couple of years later, the monks even supplemented their diet with 240 pounds of bear meat.[46]) Other purchases in 1874-1875 included 200 pounds of snuff for $166, and 306 kegs of beer for $536.[47]

Although the monastery's meals became more varied, by all accounts Johnnie Bread continued to form a major part of the Collegeville diet. The slice of dry bread at three o'clock remained a standard part of the student's day well after the turn of

When the Franciscans could no longer provide enough sisters to staff the Saint John's kitchens, Abbot Baldwin sought replacements from the Benedictines of Cristo Rey de Guadalupe in Mexico. Before the last of the German nuns left in 1958, they spent a short period training their successors in the fine art of creating Johnnie Bread, or, in this case, Johnnie Bread rolls. The Mexican sisters must have found the Minnesota winters horrific and clearly suffered significant culture shock. After a few years, the sisters retreated, and the abbot turned to a permanent lay staff. (Photo courtesy of Saint John's Abbey Archives)

Johnnie Bread was as much a part of a properly set table in the Saint John's Student Refectory in 1894 as plates and glasses. In contrast to today's individualistic cafeteria style, students ate together along with their prefects, with food served at the tables home-style. Until about 1906, the student dining room followed monastic tradition by having a prefect read an "instructive book" aloud from the lectern (on the left) while the assemblage ate. (Photo courtesy of Saint John's Abbey Archives)

the century, and Abbot Baldwin Dworschak remembered that in the 1920s, "bread was there for every meal and there was plenty of butter . . .you could make a meal of it."[48] If the patterns stayed relatively close to Father Alexius' account of the early days, it is reasonable to conclude that the young men at Saint John's ate one half to a full loaf of bread per day well into the twentieth century. Given the size of the loaf produced by Brother William, this means that they would have consumed 1,200 to 2,400 calories in bread each day. To put this in perspective, a person could meet the recommended servings for the entire bread and cereal food group in the 1990s by consuming 400 to 800 calories worth of a bread like Brother William's, or about one-third of what Saint John's students ate earlier in the century.

Bread consumption no doubt declined as the twentieth century wore on, but the affection for the famous loaf remained constant. In 1958, Father Herbert Bursinger recalled carrying the freshly sliced bread, stacked half a loaf high with the heel on top, to the dining tables where "everybody was fighting for the heel of the loaf. Most of the boys liked the crust at the top of the loaf." Furthermore, as Father Herbert noted, "When the boys went home for Christmas, each one took along a loaf of bread."[49] Even in far-away Hollywood, *Dragnet* star Jack Webb fondly recalled his days of military training at Saint John's during World War II, concluding, "there's no doubt in my mind that Saint John's Bread is the world's greatest."[50]

By mid-century, Brother William's Johnnie Bread was not only a staple of life at Saint John's, but had become a legend among those who were familiar with the campus. It was clearly time to seek a broader audience.

Saint John's University initially offered theological training and classical liberal arts but in 1872 added the Commercial Department to meet the demand for training in business. By 1887, when this photo of faculty and students was taken, the Commercial Department was thriving. Open to eighth-grade graduates, it offered bookkeeping, commercial law, and business correspondence. Despite this utilitarian emphasis, the author of the catalog argued that "a few years would be spent to advantage at the university if nothing else were learned but to converse and deport oneself with the dignity and propriety of a Christian gentleman." (Photo courtesy of Saint John's University Archives)

Notes

1. Alexius Hoffmann, "History of Saint John's," p. 56, unpublished typescript in Abbey Archives, Box 30, Historical Documents.
2. Judith and Evan Jones, *The Book of Bread*, New York: Harper and Row, 1982, p. 16.
3. H.E. Jacob, *Six Thousand Years of Bread: Its Holy and Unholy History*, New York: Doubleday, Doran and Company, 1944, pp. 142, 307.
4. This situation was re-inforced in the medieval and early modern period by guild restrictions that prevented rural bakers from producing white bread. Stephen Mennel, *All Manners of Food*, Oxford: Basil Blackwell Inc., 1985, p. 303; Hazelton, Nika S., *Cooking of Germany*, New York: Time, Inc., 1969, p. 168.
5. In the 1860s, changes in tariff laws and agricultural innovations made wheat flour much more accessible in southern Germany. H.E. Jacob, p. 294.
6. Herm Sittard, "Saint John's Bread Gets Big Reception," Minneapolis *Star*, August 8, 1958, p. 12.

By the 1903/1904 school year, when this photo of students and prefects was taken in front of the abbey church (now the Great Hall), Saint John's University enrolled thirty-two seminarians and 278 in the other units of the university. To cope with "continual indoor life," Saint John's hired its first coach and physical education director, Mr. Peter Boquel of Pennsylvania. Boquel offered "physical culture" in the gymnasium and began coaching athletic teams. Another Saint John's tradition was thus begun. (Photo courtesy of Saint John's University Archives)

7. Omer Kline, OSB, "An Historical Narrative: The Saint Vincent Archabbey Gristmill and Brewery," 1992, unpublished typescript in author's possession.

8. Whole wheat flour contains a mix of bran, middlings, and flour. White flour is the result of a sifting process that removes both the bran and the middlings. Monks of St. Vincent Archabbey, "Gristmill Recipes," 1978, photocopy in author's possession.

9. Recipes from Omer Kline, OSB, in author's possession.

10. In 1862, Stearns County produced 100,000 bushels of wheat, 68,000 bushels of potatoes, 48,000 bushels of oats, 43,000 bushels of corn, 12,000 bushels of rye, and 2,400 bushels of barley. William B. Mitchell, *History of Stearns County*, Chicago: H.C. Cooper, 1915, p. 715.

11. See, for example, the Cash Book for 1874-75, which covers April 1874 through May 1875. Abbey Archives, FVA 166.

12. There are no records on what was grown, but even if the monks had used all of their land for rye, a good year would have produced 1,800 bushels of rye at a time when the Order was buying 1,200 bushels of wheat. The estimate of cultivated land at Collegeville in the 1870s is from Father Paul Schweitz, conversation with author, September 1995. Father Paul notes that another eighty acres were devoted to hay. This is only for Collegeville and ignores 1,000 acres that the abbey cultivated at West Union from the mid-1880s through 1901. See Colman Barry, *Worship and Work*, Collegeville: Saint John's Abbey, 1956, p. 152.

By 1921 when Father Alcuin Deutsch, OSB, was elected abbot, Saint John's had grown to over 160 monks and almost 500 students in the various branches of the university. The substantial construction required to accommodate this growth is apparent in this 1924 aerial view from the southwest. A shortage of dormitory space led to the construction of Benet Hall (upper center) in 1921. Engel Hall (left center), built in 1910, gave modern facilities to the sciences, while a baseball field (upper right) sits where the new Science Hall will be. The Old Gymnasium (1901), still in front of Engel, awaits its 1937 move to the west. (Photo courtesy of Saint John's Abbey Archives)

13. Herm Sittard, "Saint John's Bread Takes a Tradition to Grocery Stores," Minneapolis *Star*, July 12, 1958, p. 5.

14. Robert Frame, Minnesota Flour Milling Research File, Minnesota Historical Society, Box 2, "Stearns"; William B. Mitchell, *History of Stearns County*, Chicago: H.C. Cooper, p. 1319.

15. This mill was built along side a new sawmill, replacing the sawmill that burnt in 1873. Father Alexius Hoffmann says that the flour mill was completed in June 1875, but the account books show income earned from it in October 1874. Alexius Hoffmann, "Chronicle of Saint John's: Buildings, Grounds, etc," and "History of Saint John's," p. 98, unpublished typescripts in Abbey Archives, Box 30, Historical Documents, Alexius Hoffmann, "Notes," Abbey Archives; Cash Book for 1874-75, FVA 166.

16. Robert Frame, Minnesota Flour Milling Research File, Minnesota Historical Society, Box 2, "Stearns."

17. See entry for May 12, 1881, in Account Book, "Cash" 1876-1881, Abbey Archives, FVA 6

18. Allen to Gentlemen, June 28, 1918, Abbey Archives, FVA 151.

19. Robert Frame, Minnesota Flour Milling Research File, Minnesota Historical Society, Box 3, "US Census-1880."

20. Father Alexius Hoffmann, "History of Saint John's," p. 259, unpublished typescript, Abbey Archives, Box 30, Historical Documents

As usual, Johnnie Bread occupied a prominent spot in the middle of the table when Father Dunstan Tucker, OSB (far right) ate with students in the 1930s. Like Father Walter, Father Dunstan (1898-1985) played many roles at Saint John's over the decades. A Dante scholar who chaired the English Department, Father Dunstan also published articles on liturgy and served as the chief academic officer of the university in the late 1950s and 1960s. His greatest passion, however, may have been for the baseball team, which he coached to great success over eighteen seasons. (Photo courtesy of Saint John's University Archives)

Alexius Hoffmann; Financial statements for 1917-1920 and 1921-1922, Abbey Archives, FVA 151.

21. Report of the Farm and Shops Commission, May 25, 1953, Abbey Archives, Farm, 20:64.1

22. "To Be Sold By Commercial Bakers," *Record*, June 13, 1958, p. 1.

23. Interview with Father Florian Muggli, July 6, 1995; Interview with Dr. Betty Sullivan, August 26, 1996.

24. Robert Gavin, "It's Got Strength," *Record*, January 12, 1948, p. 3. The current Saint Vincent's recipe calls for water and no shortening. There is no assurance that this duplicates the original, but since Saint Vincent's has insisted on authenticity in continuing to use flour from soft wheat, it seems likely that it is close. Recipes from Omer Kline, OSB, in author's possession.

25. Baldus was preceded as cook by Brother Roman Veitel (c. 1856-8) and Brother Clement Wirtz (c. 1859-1869).

26. Thomas Whitaker, OSB, "The Brothers of Saint John's Abbey, *Scriptorium*, December 1953, p. 76; Herm Sittard, p. 5.

27. Thomas Whitaker, OSB, p. 76; "The ALA Picnic," *Record*, June 1892, p. 142. It is perhaps a measure of Brother William's stature that he is one of only two Brothers mentioned anywhere in Father Alexius Hoffmann's *Sketch*.

28. Reger's handwritten answers on Sittard to Reger, January 15, 1961, Abbey Archives, 320, Herm Sittard.

29. Thomas Whitaker, OSB, "The Brothers of Saint John's Abbey, *Scriptorium*, December 1953.

30. Brother William Baldus died at Saint John's on December 12, 1918. Father Alexius Hoffmann, "History of Saint John's," p. 275, unpublished typescript, Abbey Archives, Box 30, Historical Documents Alexius Hoffmann; Notice of death from *Benedictine Forum*, February 26, 1919, Abbey Archives, Brother William Baldus file.

31. Abbey Archives, Account Book, FVA 35. There were approximately thirty different men who served in the kitchen in 1896-1897.

32. Eight more came in September. Alexius Hoffmann, *Saint John's University: A Sketch of Its History*, Collegeville: Record Press, 1907, p. 133.

33. Alexius Hoffmann, "Chronicle of Saint John's: Buildings, Grounds, etc," p. 19-20. See also Marcia Lavine and Thomas Williams, OSB, "Saint John's Furniture, 1874-1974," (exhibit guide), October 1974, p. 11. Abbey Archives.

34. Father Alexius Hoffmann, p. 19.

35. Sister M. Patricia Forrest, *Prairie Praise*, Hankinson, North Dakota: Sisters of St. Francis, 1977, p. 29.

36. Sister M. Patricia Forrest, *Prairie Praise*, p. 206-208.

37. "Local News," *Record,* October 1913, p. 388.

38. Interview with Sister Gertrude Sperr, October 1995.

39. Sister M. Patricia Forrest, *Prairie Praise*, p. 38.

40. Baldwin to Rev. Mother Maria Placida, OSB, October 20, 1955, Abbey Archives, Z 119, Mexican Sisters.

41. Herm Sittard, p. 5.

42. Clarius to Rev. Louis Munoz, April 13, 1959, Abbey Archives, Z 119, Mexican Sisters.

43. Clarus to Rev. Madre, January 20, 1962, Abbey Archives, Z 119, Mexican Sisters. (Translation by Rob Buffington)

44. Father Colman Barry, *Worship and Work*, p. 57

45. From April 1874 through March 1875, the abbey purchased seven oxen, nineteen calves, and forty-two cattle, most of which were listed as steers. Butter purchases averaged eighty-five pounds per month. Cash Book, 1874-1875, Abbey Archives, FVA 166.

46. Purchased at .09/lb from J. Young, December 13, 1877, Account Book, 1876-1881, Abbey Archives, FVA 6.

47. The amount of beer is an approximation based on the 1881 price of eight kegs for $14.

48. Father Alexius Hoffmann, *Saint John's University: A Sketch of Its History*, p. 51; Interview with Abbot Baldwin Dworschak, June 27, 1995.

49. As quoted in Herm Sittard, "Saint John's Bread Takes a Tradition to Grocery Stores," Minneapolis *Star,* July12, 1958, p. 5.

50. Webb as quoted in "Jack Webb Writes," *Saint John's Magazine*, spring, 1968, inside back cover.

When he was elected abbot in December 1950, Father Baldwin Dworschak, OSB, had spent thirty of his forty-six years in Collegeville, beginning as a preparatory school student. Despite extensive experience as an English teacher, prefect, dean, prior, and finally coadjutor with the ailing Abbot Alcuin, Father Baldwin could hardly have predicted the tumult that would occur during his term. By commissioning architect Marcel Breuer to design a new abbey church as part of a hundred-year building plan for Saint John's, the abbot launched what one writer called, "the most exciting architectural story since the building of the great medieval churches." Breuer's shocking abbey church was barely finished when the reforms of the Second Vatican Council began the transformation of Catholic practice. A voting delegate at the final session of the Council in 1965, Abbot Baldwin was credited with Americanizing monastic life at Saint John's, including winning official approval from the Vatican to conduct prayers in English. A close friend and long-time walking companion of Father Walter's, Abbot Baldwin supported the bread program while worrying about the identification of Saint John's with a commercial venture. (Photo courtesy of Saint John's Abbey Archives)

Chapter Two

To the Marketplace

The "Placid 1950s" were anything but in Collegeville, as the new Abbot, Baldwin Dworschak, sought to address the shortage of space for an expanding student and monastic population. Seeking to avoid a piecemeal response, Abbot Baldwin invited twelve leading architects to prepare a comprehensive building plan for Saint John's. Hungarian-born and Bauhaus-trained Marcel Breuer was ultimately chosen, submitting his vision in

early 1954. Moving quickly, the community began the first Breuer-envisioned project, a new monastic residence wing, that spring. The second phase was to be the construction of a new abbey church, which would begin in 1958. The estimated cost of completing the entire Breuer plan was put at a prohibitive eight million dollars, so it was clear that the search for funds would be

By the early 1950s, Saint John's had changed in significant ways: the sixty-six-member faculty included a dozen laymen, and university enrollment was over 900. Adding in approximately 200 preparatory school students while subtracting day students, one observer estimated that the kitchens prepared 3,000 meals per day and baked 280 loaves of bread. While the Collegeville population had grown, the physical plant looked much as it had for decades. Saint Mary's Hall (far right) was ready in 1951 to provide new dormitory space, but, as this view from the east reveals, most of the land to the east and west of the Quadrangle was little changed from earlier years. The entrance road (lower center) would soon give way to the new abbey church and other Marcel Breuer-designed buildings such as Alcuin Library and the Science Hall. Likewise, the farm area (upper right) would disappear and, with it, a century's worth of pride in "self-sufficiency provided by gardens, orchards, greenhouses, flour mill, butcher shop, dairy, pasteurization unit, apiary, sawmill, maple sugary, candle factory, bakery, carpenter and blacksmith shops." The barn, other outbuildings, and the 1918 flour mill (upper right next to the light-colored building) would all be torn down during the 1950s. Joe Hall (far right), built as a bunkhouse in 1923, would become a dorm before being moved in 1992 to make way for Sexton Commons, the long-awaited Student Union. (Photo courtesy of Saint John's University Archives)

a long-term affair. As Abbot Baldwin noted, however, "what are a few generations to Benedictines."[1]

While the abbot emphasized the long view, at least one monk, Father Walter Reger, was energetically searching for new revenues to meet the challenge of abbey and university growth. The man who would be known to many as "Mr. Saint John's" first came to Collegeville in 1908 as a fourteen-year-old preparatory school student.[2] After making solemn vows as a monk in 1915 and ordination to the priesthood in 1921, he did graduate work in history at the University of Minnesota and later at Columbia University in New York. During his long career at Saint John's, Father Walter played many roles. In addition to teaching European history for thirty-six years, he wore prefect and dean's hats for both the prep school and university and ultimately became Saint John's first alumni director. He also was a long time violinist in the university orchestra, served as the school's delegate to the Minnesota Intercollegiate Athletic Conference, and represented his confreres on the Monastery's Senior Council for ten years.[3]

Beyond these official tasks, Father Walter was in the middle of much of the intellectual ferment that took place behind the "Pine Curtain." As befitted a "person who got most of his education through people rather than books," Father Walter's office was "a meeting place for the literati who stopped at Collegeville."[4] Conversations with Mortimer Adler and Robert Hutchins no doubt inspired him to take a key role in transforming Saint John's from a seminary and business school into a liberal arts college, while visits with Dorothy Day, Peter Maurin, and others fueled his dialogues with Father Virgil Michel.[5] According to Father Alfred Deutsch, Father Virgil's pioneering ideas on liturgy and social issues frequently grew out of exchanges between the two men. Father Virgil would get Father Walter started on a topic and then listen, "sifting the valuable and setting aside the irrelevance." Then, after more thought and refinement, Father Virgil would prepare another of his pathbreaking essays.[6]

While Father Walter "could spout out words like a broken water main," he more often than not played the role of appreciative audience, for he "loved to visit and loved to listen."[7] As one colleague remembered, "we would have some beer and Johnnie Bread and this [donated] duck or pheasant and tell stories. . . . No matter how many times Walter had heard a good story, he would just roar, and he would laugh so hard he'd cry."[8] Equally warm and compassionate with students, Father Walter was known to gener-

Father Walter Reger, OSB, first came to Collegeville in 1908 as a fourteen-year-old freshman in the preparatory school. Continuing his studies in the university, he joined the monastery in 1915, just a few days before his twenty-first birthday. Ordination followed in 1921, about the time this photograph was taken. (Photo courtesy of Saint John's Abbey Archives)

As teacher and administrator, Father Walter always had time for conversation, giving and receiving information from "every assortment of persons—from the lonely night janitor who tramped through corridors sniffing for smoke, the alumnus with a billfold load of children's pictures, to mothers of students who were not doing well in classes, athletic coaches who always listened, to monks who happened in for the day to buy some clothes in the tailor shop, casual visitors with no attachment to Saint John's." This propensity continually interfered with the reading he always meant to do, so colleagues remembered him constantly surrounded by half-read medieval history books and stacks of recent magazines. (Photo courtesy of Saint John's Abbey Archives)

ations of Johnnies as a man who always had time to talk, whether it was to discuss a possible vocation, or simply to renew acquaintances at Homecoming.[9] Wherever Father Walter went, he had his pipe or preferably a good cigar. Peg Gagliardi, whose Collegeville home was often the destination for groups of monks, recalled "he was a chain smoker with a cigar; it was like it was glued to him. And it was awful and messy with that chewed-on end and the smell."[10] Father Walter got so involved in his conversations that he would frequently forget about the match he had struck to light his pipe or cigar until it singed his fingers. He would then fling the match toward the nearest wastebasket without missing a beat in the story, or making sure that the flame was extinguished. Only quick action by Isabelle Durenberger, who frequently donated her time to alumni projects and eventually served as Father Walter's secretary, saved the Quadrangle from catastrophic fire on numerous occasions.[11]

No matter what particular job title he carried, Father Walter was always soliciting money, and in this his excellent rapport with former students was most helpful. As Fred Hughes (SJU '31) recalled, "when you wondered early on whether you should give twenty-five dollars or fifty dollars, if you thought of Walter, the school got the extra twenty-five."[12] While Father Walter was slowly building an alumni base in the 1940s, he got a lot of volunteer help from George and Isabelle Durenberger, but little encouragement from Abbot Alcuin Deutsch. The abbot had nothing but scorn for a monk who would beg and objected to Father Walter missing evening prayers while on visits to alumni. Furthermore, since Father Walter didn't drive, his absence meant that he had drawn some other monk away from his religious duties as well.[13] Finally, however, in the late 1940s, Abbot

Isabelle Durenberger (right) helped with alumni work for years before she became a paid employee in the Development Office. Fred Hughes and others praise her for saving Saint John's from catastrophic fire by extinguishing Father Walter's carelessly discarded matches, while many visitors remember her Flynntown home as both a center of hospitality and the site of a critical bathroom. Isabelle recalls, "We used to talk about Saint John's as two thousand acres, one women's bathroom, and a bowling alley. In those days, they had only one bathroom for women on the whole campus and the guys would bring their wives to football games. They'd say, 'I gotta go to the bathroom,' and it was embarrassing. Where do you go? Over here [at the Durenberger's home in Flynntown]." (Photo courtesy of Saint John's Abbey Archives)

Alcuin grudgingly agreed to break tradition by asking the alumni for help in constructing a much-needed new dormitory. Working with newly formed alumni committees to solicit small gifts from hundreds of former Johnnies, Father Walter spearheaded Saint John's first fund-raising campaign, raising the money to build Saint Mary's Hall.[14]

Buoyed by that success but knowing that more than alumni dollars were necessary, Father Walter continued to search for ways to build Saint John's and to keep it affordable for students. "You got any new ideas today," he would ask. "Have you thought of how you can make some money on something or how you can save something?"[15] The results of this relentless search were eclectic. For example, in the early 1950s, he developed a program to make a four-inch-long rosary that attached to a car steering wheel so a person could keep track of his or her prayers yet drive safely.[16] Although that effort didn't break even, Father Walter persisted, "looking for that gold mine that would make a lot of money so we could do a lot of good things."[17] Late in 1957, Father Walter asked his friend, Canadian philosopher and media critic Marshall McLuhan, for suggestions on how to turn the abbey's farm into an asset. McLuhan, who had created a firm called Idea Consultants to provide outsider solutions to business problems, responded in April 1958 with the name of a person who "could give Collegeville a productive set up that would be noted as well as enormously profitable."[18] Before Father Walter could act, however, the abbey decided to liquidate the farm. While cows for cash didn't fly, Father Walter was much more successful squeezing money out of bread.

Father Walter's friendship with legions of students eventually led him into Alumni Association affairs. The association had existed for decades but met only at Homecoming and "did not take itself seriously." That began to change under the guidance of Athletic Director George Durenberger (SJU '28) as executive secretary and Father Walter as national secretary. An alumni directory was created in 1948 to connect the more than 11,000 who had attended Saint John's, and groups of Johnnies were encouraged to form local chapters, which met frequently. These changes laid the groundwork for sustained alumni contributions to Saint John's. (Photo courtesy of Saint John's Abbey Archives)

Getting Started

As early as 1951, Graham McGuire, president of Lakeland Bakery of Saint Cloud, suggested using Johnnie Bread to help pay for the construction of Saint Mary's Hall.[19] McGuire, who had been introduced to Father Walter by a Saint John's alumnus, thought that if the campus-baked loaf could be replicated, wholesale bakers looking for a new product would be happy to pay Saint John's a significant royalty.[20] Although McGuire's early suggestions evidently fell on deaf ears, he persisted, raising the issue several times until Father Walter responded affirmatively in the fall of 1957.[21] While Father Walter was no doubt tempted by the thought of outside revenue, he was also motivated by a sincere desire to provide the public with a quality product. In his view, the standard commercial white loaf "was hardly bread" and, therefore, "shouldn't be on the market."[22] Further buttressed by the appreciative response he got from alumni and friends when he delivered Johnnie Bread on his fund-raising trips, Father Walter was convinced that following McGuire's advice would be both good for Saint John's and a boon for the consumer.[23]

Graham McGuire (on left), an award-winning wood sculptor in his spare time, was also a very adept businessman who more than tripled the size of his Saint Cloud Lakeland Bakery in the first ten years after he bought it in 1945. McGuire was introduced to Father Walter by Dr. James O'Keefe (SJU '36), who was a good friend of both. Father Walter's efforts to create an endowment for Saint John's touched a responsive chord in the baker. Seeing a way to aid the university while increasing Lakeland's profits, McGuire pushed Father Walter to franchise Johnnie Bread and then supplied contacts and expertise as the commercial program began. (Photo from the Myron T. Hall Collection, Stearns County Historical Society, St. Cloud, Minnesota)

Once Father Walter agreed, McGuire, who "never lacked confidence in his own judgement," immediately plunged ahead, enlisting the help of his contacts at Russell-Miller Milling Company of Minneapolis.[24] Dr. Betty Sullivan, the firm's chief chemist, was given the Saint John's recipe and asked to develop a product that could be produced in commercial bakeries without losing the taste of the original. Dr. Sullivan didn't have any connection with Saint John's, but she liked McGuire and was pleased by the prospect of helping to raise scholarship funds, so she donated her time.[25] By early 1958, she had not only succeeded in creating a mix for the dark bread but also came up with a companion white bread.[26] In the meantime, McGuire worked out an oral agreement with his friend William Heegaard, Russell-Miller's vice-president, whereby the milling company would give Saint John's legal control over the bread formulas in return for being named exclusive producers of the mix.[27]

Throughout the spring of 1958, McGuire continued his efforts to make the commercial sale of Johnnie Bread a reality. As early as February, McGuire had committed his own Lakeland Bakery to production of the new loaf.[28] At his urging, the abbey soon reached franchise agreements with wholesale bakers in the other major local markets: Zinsmaster Baking Company, which covered Minneapolis, Saint Paul, and Duluth, the Rochester Bread Company, and Tender-Krust in Eau Claire, Wisconsin. McGuire also used his contacts to provide other essential services. The Stockinger Advertising Company of Saint Cloud began in late February to develop art work and labels; much of

Dr. Betty Sullivan, a food chemist at Russell-Miller Milling, transformed the classic Collegeville recipe into a mix that could be produced in commercial bakeries and invented the companion white bread that was sold under the Saint John's label. About a decade after this photo was taken, she applied her expertise to Johnnie Bread and earned Father Walter's affection. Following her retirement in 1967, she served as a consultant for many years, specializing in assistance to countries in Africa and Asia. (Photo courtesy of Dr. Betty Sullivan)

the early work was done gratis. McGuire also convinced John Ahern of Rap-in-Wax Paper Company to waive design and production costs on the first wrappers for the loaves in return for designation as the exclusive supplier, and to pay a royalty to Saint John's of two percent of the price of the wrappers sold.[29] McGuire even volunteered to supervise a limited number of franchises when production began.

Virtually all of this early development proceeded with little attention to the legal details that typically characterize business enterprises. Although unusual, it certainly suited Father Walter's tendency to "make contracts with a handshake," as well as the personal nature of McGuire's contacts.[30] In this environment, the formal agreement between Saint John's and Russell-Miller was still being drafted late in 1958, and all but one of the early franchises began production on the basis of oral agreements.[31] Arrangements with Rap-in-Wax were never put on paper, nor was there an official document detailing McGuire's role. As lawyer and lay board president Fred Hughes later noted approvingly, the emphasis was not on legal protections, but on working with "trustworthy and reliable people."[32]

Furthermore, most of early efforts by Father Walter and Graham McGuire were made prior to any clear, formal authorization from either the abbey or university. It wasn't until April 1958, at a special meeting of the board of lay trustees called to endorse acceptance of a bid for the construction of the new abbey church, that Father Walter introduced the idea of franchising Johnnie Bread. The board expressed concerns about Saint John's maintaining control, but concluded that "continued efforts" should be made.[33] This was as close to a formal authorization by the lay trustees as the project received. The monastic chapter was even less involved; the first chapter discussion occurred in August 1958, when the abbot asked Father Walter to provide a brief progress report on the first month's sales.[34]

Although McGuire and Father Walter seemed to be leading Saint John's into a major new endeavor with little authorization, this apparently wasn't the case. First of all, Father Walter and Abbot Baldwin were so exceptionally close that everyone involved agreed that the abbot would have known all the details of any project in which Father Walter was engaged. Furthermore, since Father Walter was a member of the Senior Council, his ideas were probably discussed there.[35] Most importantly, there didn't seem to be any need for broader authorization because the bread project posed little financial risk to Saint John's.[36] McGuire had driven the project with his energy and expertise. What he didn't do himself, he got others to do for free: Russell-Miller created the mix, Stockinger provided design work, and Ahern developed wrappers. Although McGuire was later compensated for some of his expenses, they were small and were paid after the program had taken off.[37] Similarly, Stockinger didn't ask for payment on about $2,000 of pre-distribution advertising materials until over a month after sales began.[38] In short, the abbey and university almost entirely escaped the start-up costs one would expect in a new enterprise.

Thanks to McGuire's efforts, by July 1958, all was in readiness. Johnnie Bread was about to enter competition for the consumer's loyalty and dollars in a rather restricted specialty bread (wheat, rye, raisin, and white hearth) market. In contrast to the early 1990s, when specialty breads accounted for forty-nine percent of all loaves sold, in the mid-1950s they had barely achieved a twenty-percent market share. Within the specialty bread group, wheat breads were the most popular, with 9.2 percent of the market, but this is still a far cry from the 24.4-percent share they held in the early 1990s. True, wheat breads had gained 0.7-percent market share in the decade since the mid-1940s while the dominant white-pan category was losing 1.2 percent, but the pace of change was clearly glacial.[39] Johnnie Bread, then, would be competing for the dollars of a fairly limited group of consumers in a market that could not be expected to expand rapidly.

The Commercial Formula

The dark loaf to be offered to the public from Dr. Sullivan's mix contained the same basic mixture of wheat flour, cracked whole wheat, cracked rye, shortening, and water that characterized the campus loaf of the era, but it gained a little nutritionally by the addition of nonfat dry milk.[40] The major ingredient change, however, was more subtle. By all accounts, the Russell-Miller flour was more finely and consistently ground, so the commercial version did not contain the occasional bits of less pulverized wheat berry that characterized the Collegeville product.[41] The companion white bread was denser than the standard commercial product favored by most Americans, and had a slightly darker and heavier crust than the norm. Both loaves were premium products, priced at twenty-nine cents for a pound loaf at a time when direct competitors such as Brownberry offered a pound-and-a-half loaf of whole wheat for thirty-three cents, and some mass-market, enriched white breads could be purchased for as little as fourteen cents per pound.[42] Clearly, success would depend upon convincing consumers that the loaf was worth the extra cost.

Father Walter Begins the Sales Pitch

While McGuire was preparing the bakeries, Father Walter initiated a two-pronged public relations campaign to break through the barriers confronting the new product. Seeking to augment the Stockinger-prepared advertisements with free publicity in the form of news stories on the new product, Father Walter prepared a thousand-word promotional piece on Saint John's Bread that he sent to both Catholic and lay newspaper editors. Reflecting his training as an historian, Father Walter's approach stressed the heritage of the bread, rather than nutritional attributes or other factors. If editors were sufficiently generous with space to print the entire piece, their readers received an occasionally mythic tale about the movement of monks from Metten to Collegeville, *Schwarzbrot*, Brother William Baldus and the nuns who succeeded him, as well as details on commercial production and colorful stories about the alumni's affection for Johnnie Bread.[43] Even greatly truncated versions conveyed three central points: that the bread was unique, that it followed a centuries-old recipe, and that it had long been produced by a group of self-sufficient monks who were now making it available to the public.[44]

If the first part of Father Walter's public relations effort was historical, the second was clearly forward-looking and innovative. Even before the first loaves were baked, he contacted the wives of alumni, informing them of the impending commercial sale, and asking for the names of others who might be interested in purchasing the bread. Then, as the bread was produced in a given area, those identified received a postcard from Father Walter, announcing the bread and where it could be purchased. By initiating this direct mail approach to a receptive audience, Father Walter showed that he was at least a couple of decades ahead of his time in marketing.

To the Stores

When the first commercially produced Johnnie Bread arrived at stores on July 14, 1958, it received a very positive response. Grocers reported that their shelves were stripped "in a few hours," while Twin Cities bakery president Harry Zinsmaster commented "I have never known a specialty bread that pro-

the Loaf
that became
a Legend....

MORE THAN A CENTURY AGO, Benedictine monks from Bavaria founded St. John's Abbey and University in Minnesota. They brought with them an Old World recipe for an unusual, natural loaf of bread. It has been the "bread of St. John's" ever since. To all the thousands who ever sat at St. John's tables, it has become a tradition. Speak to any "Johnnie" and he speaks of the bread like a legend.

NOW, St. John's has adapted its famed and rare old recipe for commercial baking. TOMORROW, you will find it in most fine food stores — in the traditional rough-grain DARK loaf, and in a wonderful, full-bodied WHITE loaf.

ONLY YOUR OWN TASTE can tell you how delightful, how different ST. JOHN'S BREAD really is. It brings you all the old-country flavor and texture and brown-crusted goodness that have come out of St. John's ovens for over 100 years! Ask for it... try it... enjoy it!

ST. JOHN'S BREAD

● 1958 St. John's Abbey, Collegeville, Minnesota, U.S.A.

The earliest Johnnie Bread advertisements featured the Twin Towers of the old abbey church, along with references to the bread's Old World heritage and its popularity among Johnnies. Even though the twin spires were actually removed in 1960 when the new abbey church was completed, they continued to exist in most advertising copy. The spectacular new bell banner, though designed by a European architect, hardly fit the romantic connection with nineteenth-century Bavaria that Father Walter wanted to promote. (Courtesy of Saint John's Abbey Archives)

voked so much enthusiasm and interest."[45] To meet demand in the first two months, Russell-Miller delivered about 6,000 sacks of the mix to the designated bakers in Minnesota and Wisconsin. About forty percent of this was for the white bread formulated by Dr. Betty Sullivan, while the rest was the more traditional dark bread familiar to students and campus visitors.[46] Since one bag of mix was enough for 130 loaves, approximately 156,000 loaves of white and 234,000 loaves of dark bread were produced per month as Johnnie Bread took off.[47]

ST.JOHN'S BREAD

"The Loaf That Became a Legend"
The original recipe now adapted for use by selected bakers...sold at better stores...in DARK and WHITE loaves.

© 1958 St. John's Abbey, Collegeville, Minnesota, U.S.A.

Father Walter sent thousands of these postcards to alumni and prospective customers. A pioneer direct mail marketer, Father Walter had a good grasp of who might be likely prospects as he built his mailing lists. Each card contained a hand-written message from Father Walter or one of his substitutes inviting the recipient to try Johnnie Bread and providing details on which local stores would be carrying it. (Photo courtesy of Saint John's Abbey Archives)

This success among the original franchisees naturally attracted attention from other bakers. As much as his other duties would allow, Father Walter exploited this interest by visiting bakeries, regaling them with stories of Bavarian monks and a bread so loved by students that "you couldn't get it out quick enough."[48] Propelled by monkish charm and the potential for a strong bottom line, Johnnie Bread made its first foray outside the Upper Midwest in September 1958, as Jersey Bread Company of Toledo and Sandusky, Ohio, began production. By October, firms in Green Bay and Milwaukee had been added, as well as ones serving North and South Dakota, and parts of Iowa, Montana, and Wyoming. At the end of 1958, after less than six months in the market, Saint John's had franchise arrangements with twelve separate independent bakeries.[49]

Moving into the Big Leagues

In addition to more one-or-two-site independent bakeries, success also attracted the attention of much larger players. The first of these was the Quality Bakers of America (QBA), a cooperative with about one hundred members scattered around the country.[50] QBA didn't produce bread directly, but franchised "Sunbeam" and other labels to locally owned bakeries. As part of this franchise arrangement, QBA provided training, monitored quality control, and coordinated advertising for member bakeries. Graham McGuire, whose Lakeland Bakery was a QBA member, saw early-on an affiliation with QBA as a way of spreading Johnnie Bread while solving the problem of supervising distant franchisees. Accordingly, early in 1958 McGuire had contacted QBA General Manager George Graf about Saint John's Bread, and sent him a loaf of the abbey's product. Although Graf liked the taste and agreed to "think about it more," his response was not encouraging. Graf expected that the bread would sell well only in large cities with high Catholic populations, and pointed out that the unique shape of the loaf as prepared in the abbey would create problems for commercial bakeries. All in all, Graf concluded in February that "this is not the kind of thing for us to tackle."[51]

Despite Graf's lack of foresight, he evidently was very adept at recognizing a strong bottom line. By the end of August 1958, QBA had made a strong pitch to Father Walter to be allowed to handle the bread program.[52] After strenuous negotiations decided largely in Father Walter's favor, an agreement was reached in late November 1958. QBA agreed to pay what Graf termed "the highest royalty to my knowledge ever asked by the baking industry," as well as accepting Russell-Miller as the sole source of the mix.[53] Father Walter insisted on the latter because he felt "a moral obligation" given Dr. Sullivan's creation of the mix formula.[54] In return for a fee of fifty cents per bag of mix, QBA would recruit new franchises, help them get started, maintain quality control, and develop and coordinate advertising.[55] By December 1958, Graf was enthusiastically carrying out his part of the bargain, recommending that QBA associates explore the Saint John's franchise because it has "the possibility of the greatest lifelong specialty bread that we have seen in a long time."[56]

While negotiations were going on with QBA, two much wealthier suitors also came calling: General Baking Company and Interstate Bakeries Corporation, which were respectively the fourth and fifth largest firms in the country.[57] While General Baking dropped out after a few meetings, Interstate Bakeries, a large commercial bakery chain with plants throughout the country, sent Charles Regan to make a determined pitch to Father Walter in late August 1958.[58] Regan's official duties were in public relations, so he was most likely chosen for this assignment because he had two sisters in the Society of the Sacred Heart, and more importantly, had met Father Walter and sampled Johnnie Bread when a friend's son was looking at colleges in 1955.[59] Negotiations with Regan and Interstate Bakeries Vice-President H.E. Meyn continued into early 1959. Finally, by April

1959, Saint John's had agreed to give Interstate Bakeries the franchise for all of California and for Buffalo, New York. Later in the year, Interstate Bakeries also began supplying Johnnie Bread in Omaha, Kansas City, and Denver.

Off to a Great Start

With a contract with a major chain like Interstate Bakeries, and with the QBA promoting franchises among its members, the scope of Father Walter's dream increased dramatically through 1959. At the beginning of the year, twelve companies with bakeries in at least nineteen cities scattered across the Midwest were producing "the loaf that became a legend." A year later, the program had not only entered the critical Chicago market, but had expanded to thirty companies in at least forty-eight locations.[60] What is more, it was now available outside the Midwest in places as diverse as Seattle, Los Angeles, San Antonio, Valdese (North Carolina), Baltimore, Charleston (West Virginia), Pittsburgh, Buffalo (New York), Manchester (New Hampshire), and Biddeford (Maine).[61] Thus, although the South was largely untapped and coverage on the Eastern seaboard was spotty, Saint John's Bread had clearly escaped its regional boundaries and was headed toward nationwide sales.

Although some of the new franchises were relatively small enterprises, the increased numbers and the presence of Interstate Bakeries meant a corresponding growth in sales. From the beginnings of the program in 1958 through early 1959, Russell-Miller fairly consistently shipped between 3,000 and 3,700 sacks of the mix per month, or enough to make up to 16,000 loaves of bread per day. During the summer of 1959, the monthly average jumped to over 7,000 sacks and then nearly doubled again, running at 13,000 for each of the last four months of 1959.[62] At this rate, bakers were producing approximately 56,000 loaves of Johnnie Bread per day across the nation, thus beginning to realize Father Walter's dream of providing a readily available "quality" bread. Furthermore, with a royalty of $1.50 per bag, the increased sales meant that payments to Saint John's went from about $4,500 per month early in 1959 to almost $20,000 per month at year's end. By the end of October 1959, the net income from fourteen months of bread sales was $121,084, not a bad sum at a time when the annual tuition at the university was $500.[63] Skeptics in the business office who had scoffed at the bread project as "another one of Father Walter's ideas" were singing a different tune.[64]

Notes

1. As quoted in "New Look for Saint John's," *Time,* April 26, 1954, p. 85.
2. Father Walter was born in Minneapolis on July 25, 1894. Interview with Abbot Baldwin Dworschak, June 27, 1995.
3. "Father Walter," March 31, 1971, Abbey Archives, 598.4, Saint John's Bread Recipe.
4. "Father Walter"; Alfred Deutsch, "Recalling Walter Reger," manuscript in Abbey Archives.
5. "Father Walter"; Alfred Deutsch, "Recalling Walter Reger."
6. "Father Walter"; Alfred Deutsch, "Recalling Walter Reger."
7. Alfred Deutsch, "Recalling Walter Reger"; Interview with Peg Gagliardi, November 27, 1996.
8. Interview with Father Gervase Soukup, July 7, 1995.
9. "An Intensely Human Person," 1971, Abbey Archives, 598.4, Saint John's Bread Recipes; telephone interview with Tom Juettner, June 21, 1995; interview with Father Florian Muggli, July 6, 1995; interview with Abbot Baldwin Dworschak, June 27, 1995.
10. Interview with Peg Gagliardi, November 27, 1996.
11. Interview with Fred Hughes, March 14, 1996.
12. Interview with Fred Hughes, March 14, 1996.
13. Alfred Deutsch, "Recalling Walter Reger."
14. Alfred Deutsch, "Recalling Walter Reger."
15. Interview with Father Florian Muggli, July 6, 1995.
16. Alfred Deutsch, "Recalling Walter Reger."
17. Interview with Father Florian Muggli, July 6, 1995; interview with Fred Hughes, March 14, 1996. Father Walter also worked with Pat Rogers to encourage students to buy life insurance policies with Saint John's as a beneficiary. Interview with Father Gervase Soukup, July 7, 1995.
18. McLuhan to Reger, April 21, 1958, Abbey Archives, 320, Herm Sittard.
19. Herm Sittard, "Saint John's Bread Takes a Tradition to Grocery Stores," Minneapolis *Star,* July 12, 1958, p. 5; Interview with Father Florian Muggli, July 6, 1995.
20. Hughes to Abbot, September 26, 1958, Abbey Archives, 316, Lakeland; Interview with Father Florian Muggli, July 6, 1995; Interview with Fred Hughes, March 14, 1996.
21. Minutes of the Board of Lay Trustees, Special Meeting, April 13, 1958, Abbey Archives, 205.1:2; Interview with Father Florian Muggli, July 6, 1995.
22. Interview with Father Florian Muggli, July 6, 1995.
23. Interview with Father Florian Muggli, July 6, 1995.

24. Interview with Fred Hughes, March 14, 1996.

25. Interview with Dr. Betty Sullivan, August 26, 1996.

26. Interview with Dr. Betty Sullivan, August 26, 1996; Minutes of the Board of Lay Trustees, spring meeting, April 13, 1958, Abbey Archives, 205.1:2.

27. Heegaard to McGuire, April 2, 1958, Abbey Archives, 319, Peavey.

28. Draft Contract, dated but unsigned, February 4, 1958, Abbey Archives, 319, Contracts

29. Ahern to Reger, May 27, 1958, Abbey Archives, 314, Rap-in-Wax.

30. Interview with Father Gervase Soukup, July 7, 1995.

31. Minutes of Board of Lay Trustees, fall meeting, October 12, 1958, Abbey Archives, 205.1:2. Of ten outlets by October 1958, only Zinsmaster had signed a contract. Hughes to Florian, October 18, 1958, Abbey Archives, 320, Bread Contracts.

32. Minutes of the Board of Lay Trustees, fall meeting, October 12, 1958, Abbey Archives, 205.1:2.

33. Minutes of the Board of Lay Trustees, special meeting, April 13, 1958, Abbey Archives, 205.1:2.

34. Chapter Minutes, August 8, 1958, Abbey Archives.

35. Interview with Father Florian Muggli, July 6, 1995; Interview with Abbot Baldwin Dworschak, June 27, 1995; Interview with Father Gervase Soukup, July 7, 1995.

36. Interview with Father Florian Muggli, July 6, 1995; Interview with Abbot Baldwin Dworschak, June 27, 1995.

37. Hughes to Abbot, September 26, 1958, Abbey Archives, 316, Lakeland.

38. Stockinger bill, August 20, 1958, Abbey Archives, 317, Saint John's Bread, Financial Data.

39. "Census of Manufacturers," 1954, Abbey Archives, 315, Bread.

40. Earlier recipe in Robert Gavin, "It's Got Strength," *Record*, January 15, 1948, Abbey Archives, Saint John's Bread Recipe, 598.4; "Saint John's Dark Pan Bread" (no date), Abbey Archives, 314, Bread Formula.

41. Interview with Dr. Betty Sullivan, August 26, 1996.

42. See Ralph's Bakeries ad, *Saint Cloud Daily Times*, July 1, 1958, p. 19; National Food Stores ad, Minneapolis *Star*, July 28, 1958. A handwritten list of cost comparisons shows Pepperidge Farms' competing white and wheat germ loaves at $0.29 for one pound. No title, no date, Abbey Archives, 316, Lakeland.

43. Herm Sittard, "Saint John's Bread Takes a Tradition to Grocery Stores," Minneapolis *Star*, July 12, 1958, p. 5.

44. For example, see Herm Sittard's "Bread's Really the Staff of Life the Way Benedictines Make It," *Central California Register*, July 25, 1958, Abbey Archives, 320.

45. Herm Sittard, "Saint John's Bread Gets Big Reception," Minneapolis *Star*, August 8, 1958, p. 12.

46. "Saint John's Bread" (no date), Abbey Archives, 316, Bread Statistics.

47. Saint John's Bread Production by Russell-Miller Mills, July 28, 1961, Abbey Archives, 314, Bread Formula.

48. Interview with Father Florian Muggli, July 6, 1995.

49. Soukup to Baumann, January 23, 1959, Abbey Archives, 314, QBA 1959.

50. "List of QBA members," January 3, 1957, Abbey Archives, 317, No Title - Red Folder.

51. Graf to McGuire, February 14, 1958, Abbey Archives, 316, Lakeland.

52. Reger to Graf, August 20, 1958, Abbey Archives, 314, QBA 1958.

53. "General Comments and Suggestions Re: Father Reger's Letter of November 11, 1958," Abbey Archives, 314, QBA 1958.

54. Reger to Graf, November 11, 1958, Abbey Archives, 314, QBA 1958; Minutes of Board of Lay Trustees, Special Meeting, April 13, 1958, Abbey Archives, 205.1.2.

55. "Detail of Services" (no date), Abbey Archives, 314, QBA 1958. For a sense of the negotiations, see Reger to Graf, November 11, 1958, and "General Comments" written by Graf, Abbey Archives, 314, QBA 1958.

56. "Executive Bulletin #29," written by Graf, December 29, 1958, Abbey Archives, 314, QBA 1958.

57. Richard Walsh and Bert Evans, *Economics of Change in Market Structure, Conduct, and Performance - The Baking Industry, 1947-1958*, Lincoln: University of Nebraska Press, 1963, p. 13.

58. Reger to Regan, August 25, 1958, Abbey Archives, 316, Lakeland.

59. Regan to Reger, August 26, 1955, and January 6, 1959, Abbey Archives, 316, Interstate.

60. "Saint John's Bread" (no date), Abbey Archives, 320, Bread Contracts. By June 1959, Johnnie Bread was said to be available at 8,000 independent stores in the Chicago area, as well as in 14 chains. "Saint John's Bread Arrives," *New World*, June 5, 1959, Abbey Archives, 320, Herm Sittard.

61. "Summary of Saint John's Bread Operations," Abbey Archives, 320, Herm Sittard.

62. "Saint John's Bread" (no date), Abbey Archives, 320, Bread Contracts.

63. Minutes of Board of Lay Trustees, fall meeting, November 22, 1959, Abbey Archives, 205.1:2.

64. Interview with Father Florian Muggli, July 6, 1995.

Chapter Three

Growing Pains

While the widespread acceptance of Saint John's Bread in the first eighteen months was a welcome boon for the abbey coffers, the rapid expansion also generated a number of headaches for Father Walter and others involved with the commercial production of Saint John's Bread. Many of these problems were the normal ones associated with a new business, but the bread's success also necessitated a more direct confrontation with the unique issues raised by the connection of a religious house with a commercial product.

Concerns about Commercialism

When the abbey began bread franchising, the dominant attitude of the community seems to have been a largely tacit acceptance. Many no doubt supported it without question since it carried the imprimatur of the ever-popular Father Walter; others certainly shared his reasoning that such a commercial venture was appropriate since the proceeds benefited a worthy cause while the public received a unique product.[1] At the same time, however, there was an undercurrent of concern. Abbot Baldwin expressed this most clearly during an October lay board discussion on the possibility of forming a separate corporation to handle bread sales. The abbot was recorded as favoring a separate corporation "to protect the reputation of Saint John's Abbey, which has become known for the Liturgical Apostolate and its educational and missionary work. The abbot said that in his opinion it would be very harmful to our reputation should we become known only for the sale of Saint John's Bread."[2] Although clearly wary of commercialism, Abbot Baldwin offered a small dig at the Christian Brothers, noting that he was pleased that at least "we were selling bread and not wines and liqueurs."[3]

As profits grew, so did the fear that commercial success might adversely affect the institution's reputation. As early as May 1959, when net income had passed $50,000, Abbot Baldwin asked the lay board if they agreed with his inclination not to announce the projects funded by this income. The consensus was "that the less said about this the better and that the amount of income should never be disclosed."[4] Furthermore, Father Walter was told that the publicity should be "simmered down," and figures on the number of loaves sold and bakeries franchised should not be released.[5]

Given this atmosphere, it isn't surprising that the stories Father Walter planted in local newspapers on the introduction of Johnnie Bread generally skirted the question of royalties. Many accounts simply ignored the issue, while others somewhat disingenuously implied that a desire to share the loaf was the only motivation: "last summer, abbey and university authorities were persuaded to allow the bread to be baked and sold by commercial bakers."[6] A few press releases did note that the abbey would receive a royalty, but even this was softened in one case to "the university adds to its funds" for each loaf sold.[7] The most striking exception to the generally understated approach was a single advertisement in the *New World*, a Chicago Catholic paper. It very explicitly reminded readers that purchasing Johnnie Bread would mean "helping the good fathers at the abbey."[8]

Projecting an Image

In addition to trying to protect its reputation by downplaying the commercial benefits of bread franchising, the abbey also worried a great deal about the type of advertising used to promote the famous loaf. During the first months, this was of relatively little concern, for most of the advertisements run by local bakers were drawn from the materials prepared by Stockinger under Father Walter's supervision. As more distant franchisees took over a greater share of the advertising, especially with the advent of QBA and Interstate Bakeries, control of content naturally became a larger concern. Saint John's, therefore, insisted on final approval of all "advertising and promotion ideas and publicity material" to insure that they were "in harmony with the dignity and integrity of the abbey and university."[9] In practice, this meant that all copy used by a franchisee had to be cleared by the abbey's bread committee, which usually consisted of Father Walter, Father Florian Muggli as procurator (abbey treasurer), and the Dean of Men, Father Francis Studer.[10]

The print ads placed by franchisees generally followed the themes initiated by Father Walter. The text of an early version explained that "more than a century ago" Benedictines from Bavaria brought "an Old World recipe for an unusual, natural loaf of bread" to Minnesota. That bread had become "a legend" for Johnnie alumni, but was now available to the public. The ad copy concluded,

> "Only your own taste can tell you how delightful, how different Saint John's Bread really is. It brings you all the old-country flavor and texture and brown-crusted goodness that have come out of Saint John's ovens for over 100 years! Ask for it, try, enjoy it!"[11]

Other ads played even more strongly on the alumni affection angle even though it required a circuitous approach to target women, the presumed purchasers. One radio spot reminded women that they had heard other women talk about Saint John's Bread, and then offered the following testimonial.

> "I guess my husband's fondest memory of his days at Saint John's University is the unusual bread they baked and served at every meal. For years he has talked about Saint John's Bread like some men talk about their mother's cooking. Now, at last, I can get it for him at our grocery store. And, honestly, now I understand why he kept talking about it. It's not just a matter of loyalty to his old college; it's really a wonderful, delicious kind of bread."

The spot concluded, "That's one happy housewife's report. It will be yours, too, after you have served your husband Saint John's Bread."[12]

The Father Walter Reger Touch

While franchisees employed the standard print and electronic media techniques, Father Walter maintained his faith in a more personal touch. In a list of "things to do in getting Saint John's Bread off the ground in a given community," he included the distribution of complimentary loaves to the wives of public officials, media and religious leaders, and other prominent figures, all "delivered by me."[13] Who could resist a free loaf of bread from a charming man described by confrere as "the Father Chips of Saint John's"?[14] Although his other duties kept Father Walter from pursuing this personal approach everywhere, he did the

Whether relaxing in his room or calling on a potential Johnnie Bread customer, Father Walter was rarely without a cigar. As Peg Gagliardi recalled, "all of the monks smoked cigars, but none of them carried them all over like he did. It was like it was glued to him." Not content to simply puff away, Father Walter also considered himself a connoisseur and employed an elaborate ritual to evaluate each new batch. The final step was testing the ash, for Father Walter believed that "a good cigar holds a long ash." The best ones would hold an inch or more of ash together while being flicked toward a spittoon or trash can six feet away. Needless to say, Father Walter's testing zones were a housekeeper's nightmare. (Photo courtesy of Saint John's Abbey Archives)

next best thing by both expanding and refining his direct mail postcard campaign. Unable to keep up even though he "burned his eyes out at night under a small light scribbling away," Father Walter sought help with the postcards from his confreres.[15] Since this labor source was unreliable, he eventually hired several local women and nuns from Saint Benedict's Convent in Saint Joseph to help him produce the postcards.[16] One of the nuns was Isabelle Durenberger's cousin, Sister Elvan Drayna, who estimated that she addressed 35,000 Johnnie Bread postcards.[17]

The increasing volume of postcards was tied to Father Walter's growing data base. Rather than depending just on Johnnie alumni, Father Walter broadened his net by seeking mailing lists from other Benedictine abbeys, and pressuring franchisees across the country to send him local phone books.[18] Initially, Father Walter scoured the phone books for families with

Irish and German names on the assumption that they would be Catholic. Later, he even reviewed reports on weddings, funerals, and reunions in local papers to find the names of Minnesotans who had moved out of state who could then be matched up with phone book addresses in distant cities.[19] Eventually, Father Walter realized that class, as well as religion and regional background, defined his market. He began to ask franchisees for names of the members of athletic clubs, the Chamber of Commerce, the Automobile Club, and the League of Women Voters.[20] As he explained to QBA's Harry Baumann:

> We can make an especially directed appeal to discriminating and prominent people—professional women, wives of professors and teachers in the schools, priests and ministers, people who live in suburbia and in the higher income residential areas, etc. These are the people who will continue to look for and remain loyal to a quality product once they have found it . . . they need to be weaned away from the breads they have been buying by a personal appeal such as our postcard.[21]

Expanding the Advertising Effort

While Father Walter refined his postcard campaign, most of the other public relations work originating from Saint John's was taken over by Herm Sittard, a feature writer for the Minneapolis *Star* and former *Catholic Digest* editor, whose father had been a student at Saint John's.[22] Sittard apparently knew Father Walter before sales began, which may explain why he wrote two very detailed, laudatory accounts of Johnnie Bread for the *Star* in 1958.[23] Whatever the original relationship, by the fall of 1959, Father Walter had managed to finagle a way to employ Sittard as a moonlighting public relations aide for Saint John's.[24] In that capacity, he wrote articles on the new

Minneapolis *Star* writer Herm Sittard began moonlighting as a publicist for both Saint John's Bread and the new abbey church in 1959. The small additional income must have been helpful in feeding his twin sons, shown here eating hot dogs at the state fair on non-Johnnie Bread buns. Remembered by Lee Hanley (SJU '58) as "a notepad and pencil behind the ear" journalist, Sittard nevertheless had much more expansive and expensive ideas about promoting the famous loaf than Father Walter. (Photo courtesy of Saint John's Abbey Archives)

abbey church, but most of his time was devoted to bread promotions.

Sittard brought a much more ambitious public relations vision to the project. For example, when Sittard was hired in 1959, Schmidt Baking Company was getting ready to produce Johnnie Bread in Baltimore. Sittard suggested going beyond the local Catholic press and the "small papers" in Maryland to plant stories in the Sunday editions of the *Baltimore Sun, Baltimore American, Washington Post, Washington Star,* and *Washington News.*[25] To hit his lofty targets, Sittard offered his Washington contacts and a general approach that was more aggressive than employed previously. The central pitch was to be to the major dailies, rather than to the Catholic weeklies, even though they "may think they rate an earlier shot at the big story."[26] Furthermore, to encourage the major papers to provide a large feature, Sittard urged the hiring of a professional photographer who could shoot both color and black-and-white shots to enliven the text offered. Finally, he called for more coordination with the local baker. They needed to sign advertising contracts with the papers two days beforehand, and "it would be charming if we could time it so the bakers sent a good-looking young salesman to the feminine food editors with an armful of fresh bread the day after our story reaches them."[27]

While it's doubtful that Father Walter objected to Sittard's sexist tactics, it is clear that the overall plan was too ambitious for the monk's taste. Whether it was due to expense or to other factors, Sittard ultimately sent copy only to Baltimore's *Catholic Review,* thus ignoring not only the major secular papers, but even dropping an approach to Washington's *Catholic Standard.*[28]

Lee Hanley (SJU '58), who was news service director for Saint John's at the time, remembered that Sittard was frustrated but undaunted: "I can recall him sitting with me and picking my brain to see if he could find some angle to work Walter over and bring him around."[29] Ever hopeful, Sittard continued to suggest sweeping public relations efforts, including the preparation of an article that could be placed in magazines such as the *Ladies Home Journal* and *McCall's,* as well as "the carriage trade magazines" such as *The New Yorker, Gourmet,* and *The Atlantic Monthly.*[30] To illustrate such an article, he begged for permission to spend $300 on a professional photographer. If he could find "a real hearth oven with red bricks," he wanted "to set up a color picture with the monk manning a peel with bread on it, glowing hearth and the like...."[31] To assist, Sittard asked Father Walter to "see if you can pick out a couple of monks who look like people think monks look —perhaps a grey beard or two or a bald jolly-looking fellow who is not overweight too much."[32] The article was written, but never submitted for publication, and Father Walter never authorized an expenditure for photos, either real or staged. As the disappointed Sittard noted late in 1963, this effort was still "awaiting abbey decision."[33]

Marketing with Moderation

Even Sittard's most extravagant ideas for promotional copy were restrained in comparison with the claims of many of the era's specialty breads, which often tried to create market share by offering themselves as low-calorie or uniquely nutritious. One Johnnie Bread rival claimed that its product was so "exceptionally nutritious" that "alone it can provide the basic elements of a sustaining meal."[34] Another claimed to "build strong bodies twelve ways."[35] Father Walter was thoroughly convinced of his bread's nutritional value as well, bragging to a parish priest that Dr. Betty Sullivan "assures me that Saint John's Bread is the most nutritious bread in the country."[36] At the same time, however, he was adamant that "no exaggerated health or slenderizing or nutritional claims" be made.[37] As a result, Johnnie Bread ads were rather circumspect. The term "nourishing" was used in some, but never with an assertion of exceptionalism. The most extravagant claim Father Walter allowed was that the traditional recipe produced a bread "so hearty and nourishing that it was almost a meal in itself."[38] Notice the use of the qualifying "almost."

The Catholic Question

Setting the appropriate tone on nutritional claims was easy, however, in comparison to deciding how to handle the issue of religion. In the late 1950s, a Catholic identification hardly generated the more neutral response it receives forty years later. As John F. Kennedy's 1960 campaign for the presidency would demonstrate, many in the country remained in the grip of a strong anti-Catholic bias, while Catholics were similarly ready to give disproportionate support to one of their own faith. By deciding to link the bread's value to its Benedictine monastic heritage, rather than making nutritional claims, Father Walter had already made the religious connection relatively prominent. The remaining problem for Father Walter was how he should negotiate the tricky terrain he had created. Should the appeal be to Catholics to buy the bread as an

As the commercial sales of Johnnie Bread grew, Father Walter and the abbey bread committee insisted that advertising copy emphasize taste and the Old World connection while avoiding strong nutritional claims. This ad prepared by the Quality Bakers Association for its members is typical of the result. The nutritional angle is limited to "hearty natural goodness," while the European ancestry is emphasized both in the text and visually by placing the abbey's Twin Towers behind classic, but non-existent, cloister arches. (Courtesy of Saint John's Abbey Archives)

Baked from a centuries-old recipe brought by the Benedictines from Bavaria...

ST. JOHN'S BREAD

famous loaf of hearty natural goodness

For the first time you can enjoy famous St. John's Bread. It's a hearty, satisfying loaf, baked today for you just as it's been baked for centuries by the Benedictines. Try the traditional nut-brown loaf or the firm, new white loaf. St. John's Bread is fresh . . . delicious. Reach for it today.

Enjoy St. John's White Bread, too!

Another fine product of your Sunbeam baker

indication of their commitment to a Catholic abbey and university, or should the issue of religious sponsorship be downplayed in order to appeal to a broader audience?

Since raising money for the abbey was a central reason for the bread campaign, many, including Graham McGuire, Interstate Bakeries' Charles Regan, and officers of the Minnesota Council of the Knights of Columbus, urged that religious affiliation be made a central part of the sales pitch.[39] Father Walter responded with an emphatic "no," arguing that it would be "a very serious mistake" to make "an appeal for the support of religion through bread."[40] Such a reaction was probably to be expected from a man who had taught his students the disastrous consequences of religious intolerance in Medieval and Reformation Europe, but it also may have been rooted in his own past; in the early 1950s the Catholic and Protestant private colleges in Minnesota had begun a cooperative fund-raising approach, and Father Walter had numerous good friends at the Lutheran colleges.[41] Finally, Father Walter rejected the religious appeal not only because it would alienate Protestants, but also for fear that Catholics would recoil because "they would feel that something which is very dear and precious is being unworthily exploited." Ultimately, Father Walter concluded that religion could enter the picture "in so far as it suggests integrity and a worthwhile cause," but "we think this must be in a very unobtrusive and secondary way. The prime motivation for purchasing the bread must always be its own intrinsic high quality as to nutrition and taste and flavor."[42]

Operating under these guidelines, Father Walter consistently walked a fine line. Johnnie Bread promotional materials clearly acknowledged the product's religious heritage by using the Saint John's name, as well as including a stylized cross on the wrapper and a drawing of the old abbey church's Twin Towers in most ads. Conversely, the cross logo was de-emphasized in 1959 to avoid the impression of "trading on religion," and approved ads almost always avoided references that would have moved from the general "religious" to the specific "Catholic."[43] For example, with the sole exception of an ad in a Chicago diocesan paper that used the clearly Catholic "Fathers," the bread's source was always given as "Benedictine monks," or simply "Benedictines."[44] For Protestants with little knowledge of Church history, these terms were probably significantly less confrontational than "Catholic."

Likewise, Father Walter sought to exploit his access to the Catholic market while avoiding an explicit call for support on religious grounds. He wrote to priests and nuns across the country to ask them to recommend Johnnie Bread to their lay contacts, and requested names for his mailing list.[45] Later, Father Walter developed other techniques, such as asking his fellow religious to serve samples and distribute pamphlets on Johnnie Bread to their students at Catholic parochial schools. At the same time, however, even for Catholic audiences, the religious connection was never paramount. Taste and quality always received much more emphasis, even in private appeals.[46]

On the whole, then, Saint John's solved the difficulties of association with a commercial product by exercising restraint. The full extent of the project's financial success was not revealed, and advertising was carefully monitored for excesses that would create an image of cheap commercialism. Furthermore, on the touchy issue of religion, Father Walter steered a careful course, using his religious contacts, but always avoiding anything that smacked of a tribal, sectarian appeal.

In addition to the problems unique to religious sponsorship of a commercial product, those in charge of the bread program also ran into many difficulties common to any franchise operation. To some extent these were inevitable, but Father Walter's lack of business experience and the unforeseen speed with which the program grew added to the difficulty. For the most part, resolution reflected something other than a bottom-line mentality, and was facilitated by both gentle negotiations and advice from Father Walter's legion of alumni contacts.

Dividing the Territory

An early, critical problem was the assigning of franchises, and hence territory. The original bakers, largely recruited by Graham McGuire, signed directly with the abbey. When QBA began to offer franchises to its members, it was obliged to honor the territorial rights of these abbey-franchised bakeries. This caused some difficulty, but nothing in comparison to the problems generated by the interest of chains such as Interstate Bakeries. With plants in most regions of the country, Interstate Bakeries naturally wanted franchises for territories already assigned or promised through either the abbey's program or QBA. Since neither Graham McGuire nor Father Walter had anticipated such a suitor, they were ill prepared for Interstate's appearance. When Interstate Bakeries made its first pitch, Father Walter pleaded for time, acknowledging that the program's development had been "so rapid and unexpected . . . that we were totally unprepared to deal understandingly or prudently with a proposal of your magnitude."[47] Since the standard contract allowed for termination of any franchise on sixty days' notice, the abbey did have a legal means to transfer the entire program to Interstate. Father Walter, however, would have nothing to do with such a move. "He would have said that's not fair," Father Florian recalls, "Even though legally you can do that, that's not an honest way of doing it."[48] Father Walter, therefore, informed Interstate Bakeries' Charles Regan that "morally we had no choice" but to confirm previous commitments to several abbey franchises, even though he realized that it might end Interstate's interest.[49] While Interstate Bakeries ultimately proved willing to negotiate for what was left, a potential deal with General Baking Company, the fourth largest baking chain, fell apart because Saint John's insisted on honoring its earlier agreements rather than shifting franchises to General.[50]

The most important battle generated by this multiplicity of would-be franchise grantors involved Chicago. With 6.2 million people in the metropolitan area, Chicago was clearly a critical market. Interstate Bakeries had plants there and in late 1958 made a strong pitch for the franchise. The abbey, however, wanted to give the rights to Gordon Baking Company, which held a large, but shrinking share of the Chicago market. More importantly, Gordon was reputed to be the largest bakery serving Detroit and New York City.[51] Clearly, if Gordon came on board, the famous loaf would have a very influential patron in three of the nation's largest cities.

While a deal with Gordon made good business sense, it was even more appealing on religious grounds. The former owner of Gordon's had recently died, willing the chain to the Archdiocese of Detroit, which had in turn hired a management team to run the bakery until new owners could be found.[52] From Father Walter's perspective, this was a match made in heaven; the loaf would make money for the archdiocese, while the religious connection would ensure that Gordon Baking promoted Johnnie Bread enthusiastically.[53] Father Walter was so committed to this idea that he ignored Charles Regan of Interstate Bakeries' threat that if Gordon Baking got Chicago, "we are all finished conducting business."[54] Since this would mean the loss of Interstate's significant resources on the West Coast and elsewhere, pursuing Gordon Baking involved a significant risk. Nevertheless, Father Walter and his associates persisted, first trying to get Gordon to join QBA, and then finally giving the rights direct-ly.[55] Unfortunately, this would prove to be a significant mistake, for the Gordon Baking franchise would have a brief and unhap-py history.

Negotiating the Legal Thicket

The expansion into commercial production also forced Saint John's to deal with some much more straight-forward legal issues. Lacking experience in the area, the abbey didn't address the issue of trademarks until pushed by Graham McGuire.[56] Finally, after commercial sales had begun, at the abbot's request, Saint Cloud attorney Lawrence Hall (SJU '29) donated his ser-vices to secure protection of the "Saint John's" label with the state of Minnesota.[57] The application for a United States trade-mark was not filed until late October 1958, months after com-mercial sales had begun.[58]

While these steps were being taken, John McGregor, a San Francisco bakery owner, complained that the sale of Johnnie Bread in the Bay Area infringed on a trademarked "Saint John's Bread" that he had registered in 1954.[59] Father Walter Reger immediately brought his alumni network into play, asking James Cullen (SJU '43), a San Francisco lawyer, to negotiate with the attorneys representing McGregor for sale of the trademark in that area.[60] Father Walter hoped to buy off McGregor by offering him the local franchise, but if that didn't work, Saint John's was will-ing to pay up to $1,000.[61] The baker countered with a demand for at least $10,000, but soon dropped his price to $6,000. With Father Walter away from Saint John's, Father Gervase Soukup, acting on the advice of lay board chair Fred Hughes, quickly wired the $6,000 to Cullen to complete the transaction.[62]

Once burned in the McGregor episode, Father Walter became very attuned to trademark issues. A Chicago law firm specializing in the field was hired, chosen no doubt because it employed Thomas R. Juettner, the son of a friend of Father Walter and a Saint John's Prep graduate who attended the uni-versity for a year before entering the Navy's V-12 program in 1943.[63] Like many other alums, Juettner did substantial work for Saint John's on a *pro bono* basis, largely out of affection for the institution, but also, as he recalls, because "Father Walter could con you into just about anything."[64] Once the McGregor claim had been settled, Juettner sought to insure the legal validity of the federal trademark protection by collecting evidence of its use in all forty-eight states. Since Johnnie Bread was available com-mercially in only a handful of states at the time, this would

appear to be an insurmountable task. Once again, however, the alumni network came to the rescue. Father Walter met the legal requirements by sending a loaf of bread to an alumnus in each state, and collecting an affidavit in return indicating that they had used the trademarked product.[65]

 In the summer of the following year, 1959, Father Walter sought further protection by asking Juettner to register Johnnie Bread, the Twin Towers design, and the slogan, "The Loaf that Became a Legend." Juettner convinced Father Walter that registering Johnnie Bread would be too difficult, but went ahead with the others.[66] The Twin Towers was accepted easily, but "the Loaf that Became a Legend" was initially rejected by the Patent Office as "merely descriptive of goods."[67] Father Walter, however, had Juettner persist through a series of denials. Finally, responding to Saint John's Business Office complaints that "we have been spending too freely," Father Walter reluctantly asked the law firm to drop its efforts in October 1960.[68] As it turned out, however, Father Walter got his way. Juettner's firm agreed not to charge Saint John's for an additional filing, so the slogan was ultimately registered on the less protective Supplemental List.[69]

Copycats and Rivals

Although Father Walter was able to secure the Saint John's name, he had less success dealing with imitators who skirted trademark protections to capitalize on the connection Saint John's had established between monasticism and quality bread. In 1959, two bakeries with at best tenuous monastic ties began their efforts. Schafer's bakery of Michigan produced "St.

Abbot Baldwin Dworschak (second from right) and Father Walter (left) were never shy about calling on the expertise of Saint John's graduates. Lawyer Herbert Adrian (SJU '29) (second from left) not only succeeded Fred Hughes (SJU '31)(right) as National Alumni president in 1951 but went on to serve for many years on the board of lay trustees. Fred Hughes was chairman of the lay trustees when the bread program began and provided legal counsel for the abbey. (Photo courtesy of Saint John's Abbey Archives)

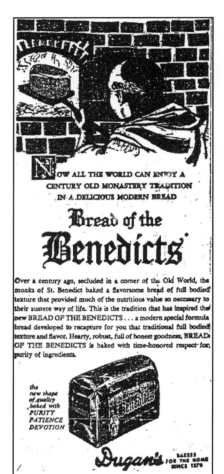

OW ALL THE WORLD CAN ENJOY A
CENTURY OLD MONASTERY TRADITION
IN A DELICIOUS MODERN BREAD

Bread of the
Benedicts

Over a century ago, secluded in a corner of the Old World, the monks of St. Benedict baked a flavorsome bread of full bodied texture that provided much of the nutritive value so necessary to their austere way of life. This is the tradition that has inspired the new BREAD OF THE BENEDICTS . . . a modern special formula bread developed to recapture for you that traditional full bodied texture and flavor. Hearty, robust, full of honest goodness, BREAD OF THE BENEDICTS is baked with time-honored respect for purity of ingredients.

the
new shape
of quality
baked with
PURITY
PATIENCE
DEVOTION

Dugan's BAKERS FOR THE HOME SINCE 1878

The meteoric rise of Johnnie Bread sales attracted the attention of others who sought to cash in on the public's apparent affection for a more substantial bread with a monastic pedigree. "Bread of the Benedicts" was one of the most blatant copycat efforts. The only monastic connection it had was a fee paid by its creators to Saint Gregory's, an Anglican Benedictine Priory in Michigan. (Courtesy of Saint John's Abbey Archives)

Vincent's Bread," which was advertised as "the Bread with a Legend."[70] Saint John's prepared to challenge the use of the parallel slogan, but the threat quickly faded as Schafer's filed for bankruptcy.[71]

The second, and more serious, effort by a commercial enterprise to exploit Saint John's territory was "Bread of the Benedicts." This product was the brainchild of Louis Ort of Maryland Milling Company, who at least sought a fig-leaf to cover his exploitation of the monastic connection. In 1959, Ort approached Saint Gregory's Priory, an Anglican Benedictine order in Michigan, about lending their approval to his project. (Ort told the prior that as a Presbyterian, he preferred to work with Protestant groups rather than dealing with a Catholic Benedictine house.) Although Saint Gregory's produced no traditional bread and Ort offered no evidence that his "old English recipe" had a monastic connection, the priory gave its approval.[72] The result was a white bread unlike the classic Saint John's loaf but marketed in a way that mimicked the Collegeville product.[73]

Attempting to use their shared religious background to resolve the difficulty, Saint John's sent Father Francis and Tom Juettner to discuss the situation with the prior of Saint Gregory's.[74] The initial results were promising, for the prior agreed to withdraw his support of Ort's product if, after study, he concluded that the "Bread of the Benedicts" was an effort to "take unfair advantage of the success achieved by Saint John's."[75] The prior, however, was in no hurry to make a decision. The issue still had not been resolved in early 1960, when Father Walter asked Juettner to drop the matter. He continued to think it desirable to "clear the market of unfair competition" but bowed to the procurator's assessment that "we might spend considerable sums without effective results."[76] Ultimately, it appears that market forces caused this challenge to evaporate.[77]

The third major effort to ride the coattails of the Collegeville success was "Monks' Bread," a white loaf similar to the companion product developed by Dr. Betty Sullivan. Monks' Bread at least had a legitimate monastic connection, for the recipe had been produced at the Trappist Abbey of the Genesee near Rochester, New York, since the early 1950s. In 1957, the Trappists began a limited commercial effort, producing bread at the abbey and trucking it to a few locations around the

MONKS' BREAD

From a treasured monastery recipe...the time-tested bread that made itself famous

mid wide green acres in the Genesee Valley, there stands an Abbey of Trappist Monks. One of the labors performed in these quiet halls is the baking of bread. Here, with the skill and dedication they give to every task, white-robed monks turn out slim, high-crowned loaves that are truly unique in flavor and natural goodness.

From a treasured Called Monks' Bread because it was originally intended for
monastery recipe the monastery table alone, this delicious bread is baked by the
Abbey's own cherished recipe. It is unique among breads.

A wholesome Because Monks' Bread is the mainstay of the Abbey's diet, it is
staff of life made exceptionally nutritious, with unbleached flour and other
most wholesome ingredients. Alone, it can provide the basic elements of a sustaining meal. With food, it adds a sturdy good taste you'll appreciate.

How Monks' Visitors to the Abbey of the Genesee were delighted with the
Bread made itself golden-crusted loaves that were brought to their table. They told
famous their friends about it. The word spread, until a brother of one
Monk undertook to sell a small amount of the bread for the benefit of the Order.
Once launched, it was an immediate success.

You never saw, never tasted, bread like this. Now for the
first time, Monks' Bread is available in your neighborhood.
The fine, slender loaves will catch your eye, on the grocer's
shelf. And when you taste a slice of Monks' Bread, you will
be won by its superb flavor and fine, firm texture. A truly
choice bread—yet the price is moderate.

White, Whole Wheat, Raisin—all delicious! Try a fresh-
baked loaf of Monks' Bread soon. *You never knew bread
could taste so good!*

BAKED IN THIS AREA UNDER TRAPPIST SUPERVISION BY YOUR NEARBY NABISCO BAKERY ·

Like Saint John's and many other religious houses, the Trappist Abbey of the Genesee had developed their own particular recipe for the bread they baked. The Trappists sold their product locally in upstate New York before Father Walter began to market the Collegeville loaf, but they didn't expand their program until Johnnie Bread's success convinced Nabisco to enter the picture. The giant baking company's advertising was remarkably similar to that developed by Father Walter, but they paid the Trappists a royalty that was only a fraction of what Saint John's received. (Courtesy of Saint John's University Archives)

state.[78] This very small scale effort was transformed in late 1959 when Nabisco, encouraged by the success of Johnnie Bread, signed an agreement to produce Monks' Bread "under the supervision of" the abbey.[79] The ads for this product were remarkably similar to those for Johnnie Bread. Monks' Bread was "from a treasured monastery recipe," formed the "mainstay of the abbey's diet," and had become available commercially because visitors to the abbey demanded it.[80] Furthermore, its promoters even stole a page from Father Walter's book by blanketing Catholic school pupils with brochures extolling their product. Despite the obvious attempt to capitalize on the positive public response to the loaf that became a legend, the Saint John's trademark offered no legal protection, and no efforts were made to seek a less formal solution.[81] Johnnie Bread and Monks' Bread, therefore, continued to co-exist.

Searching for Authenticity

Father Walter's most enduring headache came from the effort to insure that the quality and authenticity of the commercial product lived up to Benedictine—and alumni—expectations. Faced with complaints that the franchised loaf was improperly baked or didn't taste like the Collegeville version, Father Walter was steadfast in his faith that the problem lay with the bakers rather than with the commercial mix itself, and was, therefore, correctable.[82] While Russell-Miller's more uniform grinding did change the bread somewhat by eliminating the occasional bits of less pulverized wheat berry, Father Walter was generally correct. It was possible to use the mix to make a loaf that tasted like the traditional Collegeville Johnnie Bread. Indeed, in fall 1962, Saint John's began using the commercial mix in its kitchens without attracting any negative comments.[83] In practice, however, it was highly unlikely that commercial bakeries would mimic this success. The problem was that the methods used in the abbey kitchen were not compatible with mass production bakeries in two important areas. First, in contrast to the abbey's more traditional techniques, "in a wholesale bakery they use high speed mixing and they machine the dough [to shape it for baking] and with that you get a different texture even though the ingredients are the same."[84] Even more important, the loaves made in the abbey kitchens were hearth baked fairly slowly at a relatively low temperature: fifteen minutes at 400 degrees and then another forty minutes at 375 degrees.[85] This produced a compact, thoroughly cooked loaf with the characteristic thick and crispy crust that generations of students and monks had valued. Commercial bakeries, on the other hand, rarely had hearth facilities, and for economic reasons required a shorter bake at a constant temperature.

Since hearth baking was not an option in most commercial bakeries, one of the first issues was what type of container to use to bake the bread. Franchisees were told that they could approximate the dark Collegeville loaf in their regular ovens if they used screens or frames that were nine inches long, and five to six inches wide. The white bread was to be done in pans that were eight inches long, three inches wide, and three inches deep.[86] Since most commercial bakery equipment was geared to a larger size, Father Walter and Dr. Sullivan fought an on-going battle to get bakeries to buy new pans and screens rather than using what they had. The use of larger containers not only impeded the effort to maintain Johnnie Bread's distinctiveness versus other commercial loaves, but raised serious taste and texture problems.[87] As Dr. Sullivan explained, if the pans were too large, "the baker is forced to use excessive amounts of yeast food" to get the requisite number of loaves from the mix. Higher than specified levels of yeast food produced "a very undesirable flavor," while efforts to stretch the volume by adding more yeast led to a loss of the dark loaf's characteristic compactness.[88]

The other critical quality issue revolved around the actual baking. Realizing that commercial bakeries couldn't afford to follow the abbey's two temperatures and fifty-five minutes of elapsed baking time, Dr. Sullivan developed a mix that would produce a comparable loaf if baked for thirty-five minutes at 400 degrees.[89] Even so, the recommended baking time for the mix was extremely long when compared to the industry average of eighteen minutes for a loaf of the standard white pan bread.[90] As Father Walter acknowledged, "baking the dark bread is such a nuisance for a wholesale baker" because it "completely upsets the schedule."[91] Many commercial bakers were, therefore, naturally tempted to save time by cooking Johnnie Bread at a higher temperature. By setting its ovens at 480 rather than 400 degrees, one bakery was able to cut the elapsed time to twenty-six minutes.[92] This shortcut clearly saved the baker money, but at the same time obliterated what remained of the distinctive thick crust generations of alumni treasured.

Efforts to monitor quality and maintain authenticity proved difficult from the very beginning. For the early abbey franchises, Russell-Miller Milling provided the primary supervision. Franchisees were to airmail a polyethylene wrapped loaf of each type of bread to Russell-Miller once a month, where it would be tested for "flavor and taste."[93] This injunction evidently was not well observed, for in March 1959, Dr. Sullivan observed that the only loaves tested were the ones "we had

53

picked up ourselves."[94] As QBA and Interstate Bakeries entered the picture, they provided their own quality control mechanisms. Father Walter tried to insist on an independent check through Russell-Miller but eventually gave up, accepting instead a vague promise that loaves "would be available for inspection."[95] Father Walter tried to supplement this system with out-of-channel procedures such as asking an acquaintance at a Twin Cities milling company to quietly analyze a QBA loaf, but ultimately the first line of defense was a jealous alumni.[96] It was an alumnus, for example, who, outraged by desecration of the famous loaf, alerted the abbey that a North Dakota franchisee was adding molasses to the mix.[97]

Even when problems were discovered, however, rectification really depended primarily on friendly persuasion. Since revoking the franchise meant a loss to both the abbey and Russell-Miller, it is perhaps understandable that, as Dr. Sullivan rather plaintively noted, "there is little we can do but recommend to the baker how we think the mix can best be handled."[98]

Despite their inexperience, Father Walter and his associates were generally successful in overcoming the difficulties encountered in initiating the commercial sale of Johnnie Bread. Marketing strategies made effective use of the alumni/Catholic connection while avoiding a religious call and/or extravagant claims. Thanks to the help of alumni lawyers, the trademark issues were resolved. Neither Father Walter nor Betty Sullivan were satisfied with their quality control system, but the commercial product won widespread acceptance. Finally, while unexpectedly rapid growth and the abbey's insistence on honoring contracts with its original franchisees meant a rather fragmented distribution structure, by late 1959 Johnnie Bread was widely available on the West Coast and in the Midwest, while making promising in-roads elsewhere. The loaf treasured by generations of monks, students, and friends had won a much larger audience.

Notes

1. Interview with Father Francis Studer, July 20, 1994.
2. Minutes of Board of Lay Trustees, fall meeting, October 12, 1958, Abbey Archives, 205.1:2; Interview with Father Florian Muggli, July 6, 1995; Interview with Abbot Baldwin Dworschak, June 27, 1995.
3. Minutes of Board of Lay Trustees, fall meeting, November 22, 1959, Abbey Archives, 205,1:2.
4. Minutes of the Board of Lay Trustees, spring meeting, May 11, 1959, Abbey Archives, 205.1:2.

5. Minutes of the Board of Lay Trustees, fall meeting, November 22, 1959, Abbey Archives, 205.1:2.

6. "Famed Saint John's Bread is Here Now," *Long Beach Independent Press Telegram*, November 1959, Abbey Archives, 320, Herm Sittard.

7. The "university" version is in the *New World*, June 5, 1959, Abbey Archives, 320, Herm Sittard. For a clear statement on royalties, see "Bread's Really the 'Staff of Life' the Way Benedictines Make It," *Central California Register*, July 25, 1958, Abbey Archives, 320, Herm Sittard.

8. Ad in Chicago *New World*, June 5, 1959, Abbey Archives, 320, Herm Sittard.

9. Reger to Graf, November 11, 1958, Abbey Archives, 314, QBA 1958. Members of the Lay Board of Trustees were also adamant on this point. Minutes of the Lay Board, fall meeting, October 12, 1958, Abbey Archives, 205.1:2.

10. Reger to Lovett, November 18, 1960, Abbey Archives, 320, Herm Sittard; Interview with Father Francis Studer, July 20, 1994.

11. Ad in *Melrose Beacon*, July 17, 1958, Abbey Archives, 320, Herm Sittard.

12. Text for Radio Spot, Abbey Archives, 318, Stockinger.

13. "Things to do in getting Saint John's Bread off the ground in a given community," attached to December 1958 materials, Abbey Archives, 314, Pillsbury Correspondence.

14. Interview with Father Gervase Soukup, July 7, 1995.

15. Interview with Father Francis Studer, July 20, 1994.

16. See, for example, payments to Miss Florence Anderson, Mrs. Ed Eiynck, Mrs. John Feneis, Mrs. Harold Roske, Sister Elvan and Sister Bertram. Development Fund Bread Expenses, January 1959, Abbey Archives, 317, Saint John's Bread Financial Data.

17. Sister Elvan Drayna to author, April 8, 1996, in author's possession.

18. Reger to Philip, November 2, 1959, Abbey Archives, 317, Interstate. Holy Cross was also a foundation of St. Vincent's, and had been aided financially by Saint John's during the 1930s. Colman Berry, *Worship and Work*, Collegeville: Saint John's Abbey, 1956, p. 305-6.

19. Reger to Brunnenkant, June 30, 1960, Abbey Archives, 316, Interstate.

20. Reger to Hall, December 5, 1966, Abbey Archives, 316, Batten, Barton, Durstine, and Osborn.

21. Reger to Baumann, June 7, 1962, Abbey Archives, 315, QBA.

22. Minutes of Lay Board of Trustees, spring meeting 1960, Abbey Archives, 205.1:2.

23. Herm Sittard, "Saint John's Bread Takes a Tradition to Grocery Stores," Minneapolis *Star*, July 12, 1958, p. 5; Herm Sittard, "Saint John's Bread Gets Big Reception, Minneapolis *Star*, August 8, 1958, p.

12. The first of these draws very heavily on an unsigned article published in the *Record* on June 13, 1958. Lee Hanley said that since summer issues of the *Record* were done by staff rather than students, it is probable that Father Walter planted the June article and that it is possible that Sittard wrote it. (Interview with Lee Hanley, July 11, 1996.) Evidence to support this conjecture comes from an April 1958, comment by Father Walter. When admonished that the Johnnie Bread story needed to be told in the Twin Cities papers, Father Walter replied that "this had already been arranged." (Minutes of Lay Board of Trustees, special meeting, April 13, 1958, Abbey Archives, 205.1.2.)

24. Sittard to Reger, September 22, 1959, Abbey Archives, 320, Herm Sittard. The formal agreement was not made until March 1960. See Muggli to Sittard, March 17, 1960, Abbey Archives, 320, Herm Sittard. Father Walter got the funds by convincing Russell-Miller Milling Company to contribute an additional two-and-a-half cents per sack of mix, or approximately $2,500 in 1960. Saint John's matched that sum. Minutes of Lay Board of Trustees, spring meeting, spring 1960, Abbey Archives, 205.1:2.

25. Sittard to Reger, September 22, 1959, Abbey Archives, 320, Herm Sittard.

26. Sittard to Reger, September 22, 1959, Abbey Archives, 320, Herm Sittard.

27. Sittard to Reger, September 22, 1959, Abbey Archives, 320, Herm Sittard.

28. Sittard to Reger, Summary of projects to date, August 1963, Abbey Archives, 320, Herm Sittard. There is no evidence in this document of even an approach to the other Baltimore area papers even though Sittard lists comparable aborted efforts.

29. Interview with Lee Hanley, July 11, 1996.

30. Sittard to Reger, September 22, 1959, Abbey Archives, 320, Herm Sittard.

31. Sittard to Reger, October 11, 1960, Abbey Archives, 320, Herm Sittard.

32. Next to this, Father Walter penciled in "Father Alcuin." Sittard to Reger, October 11, 1960, Abbey Archives, 320, Herm Sittard.

33. Sittard to Reger, Summary of projects to date, August 1963, Abbey Archives, 320, Herm Sittard.

34. Ad for Monks' Bread, *Pittsburgh Catholic*, October 8, 1959, Abbey Archives, 320, Herm Sittard.

35. Ad for Wonder Bread, *Los Angeles Times Merchandiser*, October 1959, Abbey Archives, 320, Herm Sittard.

36. Reger to O'Connor, April 25, 1960, Abbey Archives, 315, Pan-O-Gold.

37. Reger to Graf, November 11, 1958, Abbey Archives, 314, QBA

1958. Father Walter never explained his reasoning, but Father Florian's recollection is that Father Walter thought that an emphasis on the bread's Bavarian heritage would be a more effective hook in a crowded market than would claims of nutritional quality. Interview with Father Florian Muggli, July 6, 1995.

38. Ad in *Los Angeles Times Merchandiser*, October 1959, Abbey Archives, 320, Herm Sittard.

39. Reger to Regan, January 20, 1960, Abbey Archives, 315, Interstate Bakeries; Reger to Campbell, August 18, 1958, Abbey Archives, 319, Bread Promotion-Advertising; Interview with Father Florian Muggli, July 6, 1995. Father Walter also rejected Graham McGuire's suggestion that bread publicity be linked to construction of the new abbey church. Sittard to Reger, June 25, 1960, Abbey Archives, 320, Herm Sittard.

40. Reger to Regan, January 20, 1960, Abbey Archives, 315, Interstate Bakeries.

41. Interview with Fred Hughes, March 14, 1996; Interview with Abbot Baldwin Dworschak, June 27, 1995; Interview with Father Florian Muggli, July 6, 1995.

42. Father Walter noted that this view was supported by Father Francis Studer. Reger to Regan, January 20, 1960, Abbey Archives, 315, Interstate Bakeries.

43. Hazen to Reger, March 18, 1959, Abbey Archives, 314, QBA 1959.

44. For the former, see ad in *Los Angeles Times Merchandiser*, October 1959, Abbey Archives, 320. The latter is an ad from an Iowa Catholic paper, no name, no date, Abbey Archives, 320, Herm Sittard.

45. Examples in Abbey Archives, 316, Batten, Barton, Durstine.

46. See, for example, Reger to O'Connor, April 25, 1960, Abbey Archives, 315, Pan-O-Gold; Reger to Lovett, November 18, 1960, Abbey Archives, 320, Herm Sittard.

47. Reger to Regan, August 25, 1958, Abbey Archives, 316, Lakeland.

48. Interview with Father Florian Muggli, July 6, 1995.

49. Reger to Regan, August 25, 1958, Abbey Archives, 316, Lakeland.

50. Notes by Gervase Soukup, November 23, 1958, Abbey Archives, 314, Future Bread Contracts.

51. The assessment comes from Charles Regan. Gervase Soukup notes, "Interstate Bakeries Corporation," December 1958, Abbey Archives, 317, Interstate Bakeries.

52. Interview with Father Florian Muggli, July 6, 1995.

53. Gervase Soukup notes, "Interstate Bakeries Corporation," December 1958, 317, Interstate Bakeries; Interview with Father Florian Muggli, July 6, 1995.

54. Gervase Soukup notes, "Interstate Bakeries Corporation," December 1958, Abbey Archives, 317, Interstate Bakeries.

55. Reger to Graf, January 4, 1959, Abbey Archives, 314, QBA 1959.

56. Gallagher to McGuire, June 30, 1958, Abbey Archives, 320, Trademark.

57. Abbott to Hall, July 23, 1958, Abbey Archives, 320, Trademarks. Hall attended Saint John's University from 1925 through 1928 before entering Georgetown Law School. Saint John's awarded him a B.A. in 1929 when he completed the first year of law school.

58. Application signed on October 20, 1958, Abbey Archives, 320, Trademark.

59. Zimmerman to Abbey, November 19, 1958, Abbey Archives, 320, Trademark; Trademark Search Report, November 4, 1958, Abbey Archives, 320, Trademark.

60. Reger to Cullen, November 19, 1958, Abbey Archives, 320, Trademark.

61. Jeuttner notes for phone conversation with Cullen (no date), Abbey Archives, 320, Trademark.

62. Zimmerman to Cullen, December 4, 1958, and Cullen to Soukup, December 9, 1958, Abbey Archives, 320, Trademark. For Hughes' role, see Minutes of the Lay Board of Trustees, special meeting, February 8, 1959, 205.1:2.

63. Telephone interview with Tom Juettner, June 21, 1995.

64. Telephone interview with Tom Juettner, June 21, 1995.

65. See for example, Reger to Sauve, November 26, 1958, Abbey Archives, 320, Trademark.

66. Twin Towers application filed September 18, 1959, Slogan application filed June 22, 1959, Abbey Archives, 320, Trademark.

67. Juettner to Reger, November 9, 1959, Abbey Archives, 320, Trademark.

68. Reger to Lahart, October 27, 1960, Abbey Archives, 320, Trademark.

69. Lahart to Reger, November 1, 1960, application signed November 24, 1960, both in Abbey Archives, 320, Trademark. The trademark was approved on June 30, 1961. See Juettner to Reger, August 3, 1966, Abbey Archives, 320, Trademark.

70. Juettner to Studer, October 13, 1959, Abbey Archives, 320, Trademark.

71. Juettner to Studer, October 13, 1959, and November 27, 1959, Abbey Archives, 320, Trademark.

72. Juettner to Graf, October 27, 1959, Abbey Archives, 320, Trademark.

73. Juettner to Studer, October 13, 1959.

74. Interview with Father Francis Studer, July 20, 1994. In addition to appealing to Benedictine solidarity, Juettner tried to convince the prior of Ort's deviousness by pointing out that the priory's royalty was one-

twentieth of what Saint John's got. Telephone interview with Tom Juettner, June 21, 1995.

75. Juettner to Graf, October 27, 1959, Abbey Archives, 320, Trademark.

76. Reger to Juettner, January 20, 1960, Abbey Archives, 320, Trademark.

77. Telephone interview with Tom Juettner, June 21, 1995.

78. Meyer Berger, "About New York," *New York Times*, June 18, 1958, p. 39.

79. Ad from *Pittsburgh Catholic*, October 8, 1959, Abbey Archives, 320, Herm Sittard.

80. Ad from *Pittsburgh Catholic*, October 8, 1959, Abbey Archives, 320, Herm Sittard.

81. Juettner to Reger, March 29, 1960, Abbey Archives, 320, Trademark.

82. In a 1996 interview with the author, Dr. Sullivan was adamant that she told Father Walter and others that "the bread would be different." Correspondence from the 1950s, however, implies that she believed that a similar loaf could be produced if the commercial bakeries would follow her instructions. Interview with Dr. Betty Sullivan, August 26, 1996.

83. Heegaard to Muggli, October 25, 1962, Abbey Archives, 315, Russell-Miller Milling.

84. Interview with Dr. Betty Sullivan, August 26, 1996.

85. Recipe from Sr. Bernadette and Hildegard Kremers, July 30, 1981, Abbey Archives, 598.4, Recipes.

86. Sullivan to Reger, August 6, 1958, Abbey Archives, 314, Bread Formula.

87. Sullivan to Reger, August 6, 1958, Abbey Archives, 314, Bread Formula.

88. Sullivan to Reger, March 17, 1959, Abbey Archives, 314, Betty Sullivan; Ferguson to Huber, March 2, 1959, Abbey Archives, 314, Bread Formula; Vaughn to Reger, March 24, 1960, Abbey Archives, 315, International Milling.

89. "Dark Bread-Straight Dough Formula," August 26, 1958, Abbey Archives, 314, Bread Formula.

90. Richard Walsh and Bert Evans, *Economics of Change in Market Structure Conduct and Performance in the Baking Industry, 1947-58*, Lincoln: University of Nebraska Press, 1963, p. 53.

91. Reger to Lahart, July 20, 1960, Abbey Archives, 320, Trademarks.

92. Reger to Sullivan, September 13, 1962, Abbey Archives, 314, Betty Sullivan.

93. Sullivan to Reger, March 17, 1959, Abbey Archives, 314, Betty Sullivan.

94. Sullivan to Reger, March 17, 1959, Abbey Archives, 314, Betty Sullivan.

95. Reger to Graf, November 11, 1958, and "General Comments and Suggestions," by Graf, no date but reply to November 11, 1958, Abbey Archives, 314, QBA 1958; Notes by Gervase Soukup (no date), Abbey Archives, 317, Interstate Bakeries.

96. Vaughn to Reger, March 24, 1960, Abbey Archives, 315, International Milling.

97. Interview with Father Florian Muggli, July 6, 1995.

98. Sullivan to Reger, March 17, 1959, Abbey Archives, 314, Betty Sullivan.

Chapter Four

Passing the Peak

The sales of Johnnie Bread had surged upward in 1958 and 1959, outstripping the expectations of most associated with the project. As 1960 began, thirty companies were producing the famous loaf, and Saint John's had earned as much as $20,000 in royalties in a single month. Since this success rested largely on bakeries on the West Coast and in the Upper Midwest, Father Walter and his confreres must have hoped that the spectacular trajectory would continue as Johnnie Bread found devotees in new areas. Unfortunately, that was not to be. The total number of bakeries would hit thirty-five in March 1960, but that would be the end of the expansion. Why did the growth stop?

A market analyst, looking at the most inviting areas for expansion in 1960, surely would have pointed to the nation's larger cities. Of the five largest metropolitan areas in 1960—New York, Los Angeles, Chicago, Philadelphia, and Detroit—Johnnie Bread was regularly available only in Los Angeles, with sporadic service in Chicago. The East Coast seemed particularly promising, for not only did it have large untapped markets, but with its numerous old world enclaves and large Catholic population, this area seemed tailor-made for Johnnie Bread.[1] If the enormous East Coast market could be exploited while stabilizing Chicago's intermittent flow and giving Detroit an opportunity to toast a loaf, then surely more astronomical growth was in the offing. The reasons why Johnnie Bread never realized this potential lie both in choices made by those in Collegeville, and in larger market trends.

Perfidious Partners

One key step was the decision by Father Walter and his associates to award the New York City, Chicago, and Detroit franchises to Gordon's Bakery. At first glance, signing Gordon seemed like a stroke of genius, for the baker was a leader in Detroit and New York City, and held a strong, though declining, share of the Chicago market. Unfortunately, the performance never matched the promise. There is no evidence that Gordon Bakery ever made Johnnie Bread in Detroit or New York City, while distribution in Chicago was brief and dispirited. Gordon's Chicago plant produced the famous loaf only from January through August 1959. Their total orders from Russell-Miller came to 3,236 bags of mix, or about what Zinsmaster used in its Minnesota plants in two months.[2] Expansion in perhaps the most logical large metropolitan area was, therefore, thwarted, while the other potentially inviting markets of Detroit and New York City were never attempted.

The explanation for Gordon Bakery's failure may lie in a lack of leadership while the company was in transition or from difficulties all wholesale bakeries were experiencing in a changing market, but in Collegeville the consensus was that Gordon had simply taken the franchise to keep it from a competitor. Forty years after the fact, Father Florian recalled with some heat, "they didn't make any effort, and they just weren't honest about it."[3] Coming face to face with such shrewd tactics—or perfidy—from a company that was expected to share a religious bond literally made Father Walter sick. He was so

As procurator, Father Florian Muggli (on the left with Abbot Baldwin) controlled abbey finances. When Father Walter first began talking about selling the famous loaf commercially, Father Florian "didn't think that this could work." Eventually, however, he came around, agreeing that it was "worth trying if we don't have to make a great big investment." Once the program took off, Father Florian helped Father Walter negotiate franchise agreements while worrying about how the new income would affect the abbey's non-profit status in the eyes of the Internal Revenue Service. (Photo courtesy of Saint John's Abbey Archives)

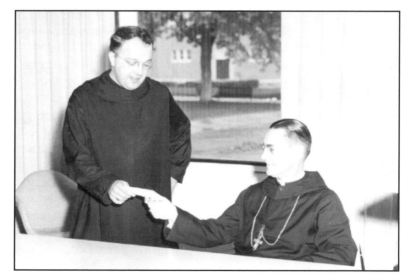

ill after one meeting with Gordon Bakery representatives that Father Florian quickly accompanied him back to Collegeville before returning alone to Chicago for more discussions.[4] Steeped in the views of his friend, social critic Father Virgil Michel, that capitalism had been become "a free-for-all struggle among men who should be cooperating as brothers . . . because of their common membership in the human family," Father Walter continued to believe that "good business was also moral."[5] When forced to confront evidence to the contrary, Father Walter struggled. At these moments, Father Florian recalled, he would "either lean on me or he'd try to find some explanation for people—for how they could be so uncharitable in his sense."[6]

Undercut by the Changing Market

The alliance with QBA, which also made eminently good sense when it was formed, also proved to be problematic. In this case, however, the key was not a lack of ethics, but rather changing market conditions. In the 1950s and early 1960s, the eight largest bakery companies greatly increased their market share by absorbing independents and penetrating virtually all of the markets in what previously had been a regionalized industry.[7] These firms had the funds for large scale advertising, and by virtue of their size, could command shelf space for their products at the expense of smaller independent producers. QBA members, in contrast, were generally smaller bakers outside major metropolitan areas who joined the cooperative to gain advantages that would allow them to avoid absorption by the giants. Without geographic position, large advertising budgets, or leverage with grocery chains, they were not in a position to insure the success of Johnnie Bread in the larger markets.[8]

Father Walter had tied the loaf's fortunes to one industry giant, Interstate Bakeries, which did provide substantial help for Johnnie Bread in the major metropolitan markets of the West Coast. Interstate's role was limited initially by Father Walter's insistence on honoring his prior commitments to the abbey and QBA franchisees. By late 1959, however, Interstate Bakeries began pressing for more. Interstate Vice-President Harry Meyn wrote acknowledging that "in all propriety and good conscience" Saint John's couldn't cancel the QBA franchises, but proposing a transfer to Interstate Bakeries if QBA didn't dramatically improve their performance within a few months.[9] When this suggestion was ignored,

Interstate Bakeries escalated, offering the abbey one million dollars for the rights to Saint John's Bread. Father Florian, one of the recipients of Interstate's bid, later believed "we should have sold it to them," but at the time rejected the overture. Father Florian and lay board chair Fred Hughes thought, "this is going too well so why should we give that up." They were also, no doubt, relieved not to have to try to convince Father Walter, who refused to even travel to Interstate Bakeries' Kansas City headquarters to hear the offer.[10] In the wake of the Gordon Bakery disaster, Saint John's did turn over the Chicago franchise to Interstate, but this was far short of what the big baker wanted.[11] Without the commitment that would have come from a unified national program, and lacking an Eastern territory other than Buffalo, Interstate Bakeries was ultimately not in an optimum position to help Johnnie Bread break new ground in the major metropolitan areas of the East.

Although a strong, nation-wide effort from Interstate Bakeries certainly would have helped sales, Johnnie Bread's expansion still might have been blunted by a second industry trend of the late 1950s and early 1960s: the movement of grocery chains themselves into bread production.[12] The creation of in-store bakeries, or the hiring of wholesale bakers to create a private label line, generally resulted in significant cost savings, which put premium products like the famous loaf at even more of a price disadvantage.[13] More important, the presence of in-house brands made it even more difficult for non-affiliated breads to compete for critical shelf space; in some cases, grocery chains limited outside suppliers to ten to twenty percent of the bread sold on site.[14] This certainly was a major barrier for Interstate Bakeries in Chicago, where even entreaties from persistent alumni couldn't get Jewel Stores to stock Johnnie Bread.[15] While the data is somewhat spotty, it seems clear that this phenomena was most advanced on the East Coast in the late 1950s. For example, while A&P, Giant, and Safeway controlled thirty percent of the Washington, D.C., bread market, in-store bakeries accounted for two percent or less in Los Angeles, San José, Fresno, and Sacramento.[16] Penetration of the major metropolitan markets on the East Coast would therefore have required that Johnnie Bread swim against a significant industry tide.

Slow in the South

Aside from the major cities of the East and Midwest, the other area that seemed to offer untapped potential for expansion after the first rush was the South. Although the major whole-sale chains controlled a large market share in most parts of the South, the region retained a large number of independent bakeries, many of them affiliated with QBA.[17] As it turned out, however, Johnnie Bread failed to make real inroads here as well.

By early 1959, thirty-two bakeries in the South had signed letters with QBA reserving their right to a Johnnie Bread franchise. Out of this group, however, only five, or 15.6 percent, ever activated their rights. In contrast, the activation rate for QBA bakeries in the rest of the country was 39.2 percent.[18] This was probably due in part to differences in ethnic heritage and bread preferences, but it also clearly involved the South's historic anti-Catholicism, which was no doubt exacerbated by the presidential candidacy of John F. Kennedy. This was certainly evident in early 1960, as rising sales brought new attention and franchising inquiries from Southern bakers. One Texas bakery asked about the possibility of using the mix "under another name that would not be so controversial in our territory," while Harry Baumann of QBA reported that another admitted that it was backing away because "we are afraid of the religious angle."[19] Father Walter wondered if such hesitancy would be affected by Senator Kennedy's apparent victory over religious bias in the West Virginia primary, and concluded on the optimistic note that "everyday as we go along there seems to be less and less prejudice against Catholics all over the country. Whether Kennedy wins or not it is a real blessing that he is running for office."[20] Unfortunately, despite Father Walter's optimism and Kennedy's victory, the problem didn't disappear overnight. Two years later, QBA's Harry Baumann remained optimistic about expansion in the East, but wrote off the South because the bread "has a few strikes against it because of the religious aspect."[21]

Losing Friends

Although Collegeville decisions, changing market structure, and religious prejudice combined to halt the expansion of Johnnie Bread into new territories, the program still would have been in great shape if it had been able to sustain the level of sales in established territories that it had achieved by late 1959. Again, unfortunately, that was not the case.

Measured in terms of sales of the mix and, hence, royalty income, the bread program reached its peak in late 1959. During the last four months of the year, Russell-Miller Milling Company delivered an average of 13,100 sacks of mix per month.[22] Deliveries for the first four months of 1960, however, were thirty-five percent lower, and by the end of the year had fallen to an average of 6,451 bags per month, or slightly less than half of what was sold in the comparable period a year earlier.[23] This meant that the abbey's bread royalties in late 1960 were a little under $10,000 per month, or about half of the return in the peak months of late 1959. Since sales had been smaller in early 1959, the overall return for calendar year 1960 was only about seven percent less than for 1959 ($133,587 to $144,396), but the trend was obviously very worrisome.[24]

The revenue decline reflected a drop in both the number of sacks of mix consumed by participating bakeries, and the loss of a number of franchises. Sales to Interstate Bakeries, the largest customer, were fifty-four percent lower in late 1960 than they had been in late 1959. Schmidts and Zinsmaster, the second and third largest, were off thirty percent and twenty-eight percent respectively.[25] While the orders from large firms fell, a number of the smaller firms simply terminated their franchises. Father Walter's program reached its peak of thirty-five franchisees in March 1960, but in the next three months, eight firms dropped out.[26] Three of the eight had never started full-scale production, but one of the defectors was Sweetheart Bakeries of North Dakota, which had been one of the earliest franchises signed by the abbey.[27]

Much to Father Walter's dismay, the downward trend that began in 1960 was not just a temporary setback. Total sales for 1961 were a depressing thirty-six percent below 1960; they dropped another thirty-eight percent in 1962 and twenty-six percent more in 1963.[28] With only 25,705 sacks sold in 1963, the abbey's annual royalties from bread had dwindled to $38,557.50, or slightly over a quarter of what had been taken in during the peak year of 1959. Furthermore, the number of participating bakeries had shrunk so severely that the potential for reversing the sales decline had evaporated as well. By late 1963, only nine franchises were still active, and the largest, Interstate Bakeries, had dramatically cut back.[29] After dropping the loaf in Chicago, Kansas City, Omaha, Denver, and elsewhere, by late 1963, Interstate continued to exercise its franchise only in Buffalo and at eleven California sites.[30]

As the slide continued, Father Walter did his best to stem the flow. He was so anxious to rescue the program that he proposed that the abbey purchase loaves from Lakeland Bakery of Saint Cloud that were too old to be sold commercially, and offered that "if it works here we may suggest using it in other areas where similar institutions to ours exist."[31] He tried to rally the alumni by asking chapters across the country to organize special bread committees to promote sales.[32] Finally, Father Walter gave up the last of his beloved teaching responsibilities in 1962 so that he would have more time to promote bread. Accordingly, when Interstate Bakeries informed him in June 1962, that it intended to drop its franchises in Chicago, Omaha, and Denver, Father Walter begged for an extension in Omaha and promised that he would now have the time to help there as he had in the still successful Buffalo market.[33]

The jaunty cigar-in-hand pose was so well known to graduates and friends that Father Walter usually received a dozen or more boxes of cigars every Christmas. Unwilling to follow monastic ideal and turn all of his bounty over to the community, he salved his conscience by giving the procurator the inferior cigars and saving the best for himself. Father Walter displayed some embarrassment when chided about this weakness but usually responded with some banter. Once, however, confreres broke through the façade by printing a fake edition of the *Record* headlined "Alumni Secretary Exposed" with an article accusing Father Walter of accepting cigars in lieu of alumni dues. The pranksters reported that he was "momentarily speechless" and then exploded into "nearly unprintable language in such a stream" that they had a hard time cuting him off to reveal the hoax. (Photo courtesy of Isabelle Durenberger)

Seeking the Reasons Why

Clearly the decline wasn't due to any loss of interest or effort on Father Walter's part. Why, then, wasn't Johnnie Bread able to sustain the success of its first eighteen months? Why did it lose sales in the areas where it had been so successful? Naturally, those associated with the project offered a variety of different answers.

Father Walter continued to insist that quality was a central issue. For example, in 1960, he complained to Dr. Sullivan that "I have had reports from friends on the West Coast that the Hansen loaves are gummy and under-baked."[34] In short, Father Walter believed that if bakers would do what they were supposed to, the quality of the product would result in sustained sales. Judging from the surviving files, however, such complaints were extremely rare and occurred over a broad chronological span, so problems with quality control don't seem to explain any significant loss of market share after 1959.

Industry figures, especially those connected with QBA, approached the problem from a very different perspective, insisting that bakers were dropping Johnnie Bread because the profit margins were too small. Since Saint John's Bread was a premium product, raising the price seemed out of the question. From QBA's perspective, profitability—hence a baker's willingness to stay with the program—required two changes. First, and most important, QBA officials lobbied for the abbey to reduce its $1.50 per sack royalty.[35] Second, they wanted to end Russell-Miller's monopoly on the mix. The hope was that greater competition would force Russell-Miller to lower the cost of the mix, and that the emergence of different suppliers would reduce shipping costs and delays for distant bakeries.[36]

On one level, the QBA argument was reasonable, for the loaf that became a legend was more expensive to produce. A confidential analysis forwarded to Father Walter showed that the cost per unit of the traditional Saint John's loaf was five and one-half cents ($0.055) more than that for Hollywood Bread, a competing specialty bread with the same wholesale price. The Saint John's ingredients were $0.027 more, and the royalty was $0.01 greater than Hollywood's. Higher labor costs caused by the slow bake accounted for the remaining $0.018.[37] While the Saint John's costs were certainly higher, the QBA argument that that factor alone caused franchisees to drop the line isn't entirely convincing. Bakers, after all, had been anxious to jump on the bandwagon earlier, despite the higher production costs, when Johnnie Bread was out-performing Hollywood Bread and other competitors. Furthermore, while the Saint John's royalty was high relative to the $0.50 per bag that the Trappists of the Genesee received, the comparison with Hollywood Bread shows that this aspect played a relatively small part in the price differential.[38]

A much more compelling explanation for shrinking sales lies in the nature of the specialty bread market. With white pan loaves dominating the field, all specialty breads together constituted slightly less than twenty percent of bread sales in the late 1950s. Since there were many different varieties of specialty breads, any one type—such as Johnnie Bread—formed a relatively insignificant portion of a baker's operation and was, therefore, unlikely to generate great loyalty on the baker's part. If sales slipped, most bakers simply picked up a new specialty loaf, and hoped that novelty, rather than sustained advertising expenditures, would be sufficient to gain customers. In short, the specialty bread market was highly competitive and very unstable, with few entrants displaying any staying power. The volatility of the market can best be seen in a survey done in San Diego measuring the brands found in homes possessing some type of specialty bread. One brand (Oroweat) did lead consistently throughout the three years covered, but no other bread was able to maintain a consistent position. In a two month reporting period in late 1960, Saint John's bread jumped from 2.2 percent of the homes to 4.5 percent; competitors experienced drops from 9.9 percent to 4.0 percent and from 6.0 percent to 1.9 percent over similar periods.[39] Most often, such declines would be enough to send the baker looking for a new product.

The specialty bread pattern of a quick start and slow decline was certainly evident in many of the Johnnie Bread markets. For example, Jersey Bread, of Toledo, Ohio, received an average of 1,170 sacks per month during the first quarter it was involved in the program. The numbers fell sharply to 283 in the second quarter and to 200 by the fifth quarter. At that point, Jersey terminated production.[40] Zinsmaster, in the Twin Cities and Duluth, also started off at a very fast pace, purchasing an average of 2,009 sacks of mix per month during the fall of 1958. A year later, the figure was 1,108, and by late 1962 it had stabilized at a little over 500 sacks per month.[41] Although both bakeries had experienced tremendous declines in the demand for Johnnie Bread, Zinsmaster continued production. Evidence is scarce, but in this case it is easy to imagine that Saint John's Bread had a sufficient loyal following in Minnesota to prompt Zinsmaster to stay with it, rather than searching out a replacement.

While alumni loyalty could help in Minnesota, how could a specialty bread like the famous loaf compete elsewhere? How could it generate enough of a following to keep a baker producing it after the novelty had worn off? One key, obviously, was to provide the same loaf to distant markets that had provoked such loyalty from those who had consumed it in Collegeville. That, sadly, was simply not possible for several reasons.

Above all, what generations of hungry alums remembered was a bread that had just been baked. As Abbot Baldwin remarked, "this was always fresh and sometimes even warm when we got it because it was baked every day and

Generations of Saint John's students and, later, those from the College of Saint Benedict grew accustomed to having fresh-baked Johnnie Bread available every day. As one explained in the year-book, "We were especially lucky, for we lived with the tradition daily, as the bread was served in plenty. Though it may have seemed we would have grown out of our taste for the bread, we never did. In turn, we generated a love for this bread within our families, for it was a symbol of the wholesomeness of the St. John's tradition." That tasty symbol came from the hands of Clem Meyer, who worked in the kitchens from 1960 to 1983, and Brother Raphael Olson, OSB, (pictured) who filled in on weekends and during vacations. (Photo courtesy of Saint John's Abbey Archives)

during the night."[42] Those who have been rewarded for making their own bread can only smile with understanding. Any bread is infinitely better fresh out of the oven, and there was no way that the commercial Johnnie Bread could replicate that experience.

Since most Americans in the late 1950s weren't used to fresh out-of-the-oven bread, however, there was still hope that Saint John's Bread could provoke loyalty, if not fanaticism, if the commercial product could mirror the unique taste and texture of a thoroughly cooled loaf of the original. While memories differ, the consensus seems to be that Dr. Sullivan's formula captured the taste of the Collegeville loaf, but that the commercial texture was distinctly different. One enthusiastic alumnus from Saint Paul praised the Zinsmaster product as "having the exact taste of my old friend Brother Bill's that I knew as a boy at Saint John's." At the same time, however, he acknowledged that the commercial version was both "somewhat different in texture," and "the crust a lot softer."[43]

To some extent, the failure of the commercial product to achieve the texture of the original was a necessary consequence of the different baking processes. With the exception of Schmidt's of Baltimore, commercial bakeries did not replicate the abbey's hearth ovens, so their product lacked the crispy, hard crust of the original. Theoretically, screen baking in conventional ovens, done "under the right conditions," could "approach hearth-baked characteristics."[44] To those who knew the original, however, the distance between "approaching" the real thing and equaling it remained as great as between a fifteen-foot putt and a tap-in. As one disgruntled alumnus put it, "The commercial version was not all that great. It wasn't that different from the regular whole or cracked wheat available."[45]

Since authenticity was a problem even under the best of conditions, any attempt by bakers to cut corners naturally made the problem worse. Using pre-existing equipment that didn't meet Dr. Sullivan's specifications, pan baking the dark bread, speeding up baking, or changing other procedures all saved money but produced a Saint John's Bread that lost its uniqueness as it became more like other wheat breads on the market. This was critical, for as Father Walter repeatedly pointed out, Saint John's Bread couldn't hope to attract customers to a higher-priced loaf unless it offered something unique.[46]

Ironically, the decision to pair the dark loaf with a companion white loaf may also have impaired Father Walter's ability to carve out a distinct notch for the traditional bread. Offering the white loaf had been a shrewd move since it accounted for forty-two percent of the mix sales during the first four years, and was certainly in line with standard practice in the industry.[47] Competitors such as Brownberry and Pepperidge Farms also included white loaves in their line, thereby offering the customer the appeal of distinctive quality but with a taste that didn't stray as far from mass preferences. Saint John's also sought the quality image, but did so by emphasizing an Old World heritage that didn't fit very well with a white bread. Furthermore, any claim to distinctiveness rested with the classic loaf, rather than with Dr. Sullivan's white bread. By producing both loaves, then, Saint John's may have undercut its ability to project a unique image for the traditional Johnnie Bread.

The Advertising Angle

With a product that didn't match the uniqueness of the original in a very volatile market, the only way that Saint John's Bread could hope to avoid the standard specialty bread pattern was through massive advertising. As William Heegaard of Russell-Miller reminded Father Walter, "The history of most specialty breads is an increase from the initial promotion and distribution but a gradual decline in volume unless there are periodic and very heavy promotion programs."[48] Why, then, wasn't the necessary marketing done?

One reason was that the advertising budgets simply weren't adequate to mount the kind of campaign that was necessary to sustain sales after the initial interest waned. The standard agreement required franchisees to spend a minimum of $1.50 on advertising for each sack of mix purchased. QBA's General Manager George Graf noted that this was "too low" and recommended a sixty percent increase.[49] Of course, individual franchisees could have voluntarily raised their expenditures to approach Graf's recommendation, but given the situation, it seems unlikely that many would do so. First of all, since the production and mix costs for Saint John's Bread were high, bakers already felt that their margins were squeezed and probably were reluctant to spend more on advertising. Second, for most bakeries, Johnnie Bread was only one part of a much broader product line. If it made money, fine, but if the public's interest waned and sales fell, the baker didn't have a deep financial or emotional investment in continuing production, let alone investing more in advertising to restore sales. Finally, the connection between mix sales and advertising expenditures trapped the product in a death spiral: each reduction in orders meant less money available for promotion.

The problem of inadequate advertising resources was compounded by lack of coordination. Many of the early franchisees used pieces generated by Father Walter and Herm Sittard. As the program grew, these and some other standard materials continued to be distributed through the Stockinger

SEE THE ENTIRE
MINNESOTA STATE HIGH SCHOOL
BASKETBALL
TOURNAMENT
DIRECT FROM WILLIAMS ARENA

EXCLUSIVELY ON
WTCN-TV *channel* 11

TELECAST SCHEDULE

THURS. MARCH-19	FRI. MARCH-20	SAT. MARCH-21
1:45 P.M.	7:30 P.M.	7:15 P.M.
7:30 P.M.	9:00 P.M.	9:00 P.M.

BROUGHT TO YOU COURTESY OF

St. John's
BREAD

While the stereotypical grocery-buying housewife probably wasn't glued to television coverage of the State High School Basketball tournament in the early 1960s, this advertising tactic may have paid off by influencing other members of the household. Whether effective or not, this kind of ad certainly must have pleased Father Walter, who was a regular at Johnnie basketball games. (Courtesy of Saint John's Abbey Archives)

Advertising Agency in Saint Cloud. QBA both bought materials from Stockinger and created advertising for its affiliates, including television spots filmed at Saint John's; in addition, individual franchisees spent their mandated advertising budgets on their own copy.[50] Interstate Bakeries also paid to develop its own print, radio, and television materials. Clearly there were numerous missed opportunities to stretch the impact of advertising dollars by coordinating and/or consolidating efforts.[51] Sittard made a few overtures toward a more cooperative effort but was rejected, apparently because bakers were committed to their own advertising firms, and those firms didn't want to risk control or revenues by coordinating copy.[52]

The marketing program was also less effective than it might have been because Father Walter's direct marketing personal touch was lost. In the beginning, standard advertising was supplemented by Father Walter's postcard campaign through his alumni/Catholic network. These efforts, when employed, evidently had a significant impact. Even as late as 1966, Red Owl officials requested that "you direct your postcard campaign into the suburban areas where these stores are located," and a Safeway baker wrote, "Please advise the Catholic organization that is responsible for the Saint John's Bread formula that we now are promoting this product in Montana and a huge key to the success of the sale of this bread is the correspondence they put out to the local Priest and Parishioners."[53] As the program grew, however, this direct marketing Collegeville role generally disappeared. Although QBA affiliates were free to spend part of their advertising budget on Father Walter's postcard barrage, the association did not encourage them to do so; the dominant approach was therefore "the regular conventional one which serves for Sunbeam or Taystee or what have you."[54]

From Father Walter's perspective, using conventional advertising for an expensive specialty bread just didn't make sense. When sales dropped, he repeatedly implored officials from both QBA and Interstate to adopt a much more targeted approach. As he explained to Interstate Bakeries' Charles Regan:

> For a hundred dollars we can get out about two thousand cards, hand-written and personally addressed, postmarked Collegeville, Minnesota and affixed with a three-cent commemorative stamp. The card will be addressed to a Catholic woman who is a nurse or teacher or professional woman or the wife of some business executive or profes-

sional person or one with two telephone numbers. . . . I hope, Chuck, that somehow you will be able to persuade Interstate to allow us here at the University to experiment with this promotion which we have developed here on campus.[55]

Like contemporary direct marketers, Father Walter had carefully delineated his market: Catholics, yes, but also upper income professionals who would both appreciate and be able to afford a premium product. One wonders what he would have done with a computer and access to huge data banks.

Despite the wisdom of Father Walter's approach, he was too far ahead of his time to move his large commercial partners. Instead of devoting resources to targeted advertising, they increasingly complained about the abbey's restraints on their sales pitches. Regan, for example, thought that it would be "a waste of time" to re-introduce Johnnie Bread in the Chicago market unless "the powers to be at St. Johns College (sic) reverse their previous attitude and decisions as to how to merchandise the product and simply turn it over to an advertising agency on a contract basis and let them do the merchandising without interference from any suggestions from the college faculty as to how they should be merchandised." "Religious fathers," he concluded, should "confine their energies to the proper operations of the church and the Catholic teaching and let businessmen who know how to do such things properly merchandise the product."[56] Given this attitude, Father Walter's unconventional approach didn't stand a chance.

Finally, it seems safe to assume that QBA and Interstate Bakeries, like the smaller players, lacked any special commitment to Saint John's Bread that would cause them to make an extra effort to reverse the slow decline in sales that most analysts expected from a specialty bread. Executives from the two firms indicated great affection for Father Walter and expressed regret when they eliminated franchises, but as one put it, "We must face facts and in the interest of good business, our actions must be dictated by those facts."[57] Since Johnnie Bread was simply one product among many, and as a specialty bread not expected to survive, they were unwilling to wait while Father Walter rallied the faithful, let alone invest more in advertising.[58]

This version of the advertising postcard, featuring the new Breuer-designed bell banner and abbey church, was developed at some point in the mid-1960s. It was not widely distributed, however, perhaps because most friends of Saint John's still identified the campus with the old Twin Towers. (Courtesy of Saint John's Abbey Archives)

75

Abbey Restraint

Clearly, the multiple problems of inadequate resources, misdirected efforts, and lack of sustained commitment could have been mitigated by a more aggressive abbey role in marketing. This effort was not forthcoming, however, for a number of reasons. Initially, an independent abbey-financed advertising campaign would have meant spending some of the royalty income, thus undercutting a central purpose of the program. Second, and more important, Father Walter lacked both time and inclination to provide centralized control. After all, first Graham McGuire, then QBA and Interstate Bakeries had been brought in to provide marketing as well as production help. Still, by 1961-62, given the decline in sales and Father Walter's frustrations with the commercial approach, it seems surprising that he didn't suggest that the abbey take on a more central role. The answer appears to lie in his understanding of the tax laws.

From the beginning, the bread program was set up in a way that largely insulated Saint John's from direct commercial activity. Rather than producing bread or selling the mix, they simply received a royalty from those who did. The only active link was through advertising, where, in a few cases, Father Walter and his staff provided as much as fifteen percent of the billed services.[59] As early as November 1958, however, people associated with Saint John's were worried that the royalty income and Father Walter's promotional activities might threaten the abbey's general tax-exempt status. At attorney Herb Adrian's (SJU '29) request, an expert, Joseph A. Maun, was asked to evaluate the bread operations in light of recent Internal Revenue Service interpretations.[60] Maun noted that income earned by otherwise tax-exempt institutions could be taxed if it "is not substantially related" to the institution's purpose. On the other hand, the statutes also said that revenues were exempt so long as the abbey or the abbey-owned corporation that generated the income were "not operated for the primary purpose of carrying on a trade or business for profit." Finally, Maun highlighted a clause that exempted unrelated income from taxation if "substantially all the work . . . is performed without compensation."[61] In short, Maun's implied conclusion was that so long as the bread program didn't become so large that it could be seen as the "primary purpose" of the institution, and as long as the work was done by monks who didn't receive a salary, the royalties were exempt from taxation.

Maun's words became much less reassuring, however, when the Justice Department filed a suit in late 1959, challenging the Christian Brothers' claim for tax exemption for its brandy and wine business.[62] While the California order was much more directly involved in production and sales, the government's action clearly indicated that the precise demarcation line had yet to be drawn. Tom Juettner, the bread project's trademark lawyer, was so concerned that he pushed Father Walter to lunch with a Chicago colleague who was an expert in tax law. After a little research, Juettner's friend, Joe Tansill, pointed out that the Internal Revenue Service had ruled that religious and charitable institutions could lose their exempt status if "more than an insubstantial portion of its activities are for other purposes." While the IRS had not defined "insubstantial," Juettner worried that "the amount of income derived from bread royalties may already have changed the character of Saint John's in the eyes of the Internal Revenue Service, in which case all of your income might be subject to taxation." Juettner recommended that the abbey immediately submit "hypothetical questions" to the IRS to clarify the situation.[63] Father Walter replied almost immediately, thanking Juettner but rejecting his solution. Father Walter noted the possible risk but concluded that he and Father Florian "feel that at least for another short while we should not call the attention of government officials to our affairs since we are following what seems to be good legal judgement at the moment."[64] Discretion, Father Florian later explained, seemed advisable since the IRS contained both friends and those "who would jump on an opportunity to crush an institution like this."[65] Furthermore, Father Walter believed that the framers of the tax code had wanted to keep exempt institutions from using their status to gain an unfair advantage against for-profit competitors but at the same time wanted them to continue to "promote the general welfare" by doing things that the government would "otherwise have to do itself." Since the "proceeds from the Saint John's Bread operation go to help cover a college deficit incurred in educating young men for society at far less than cost price," Father Walter believed "we are fulfilling properly the purpose of the tax exemption."[66]

Despite Father Walter's reassuring words about "good legal judgement," the exemption issue worried him even more after the Christian Brothers were forced to pay 3.4 million dollars in back taxes.[67] Decades later, Father Gervase Soukup still remembered the shock of a *Wall Street Journal* headline that read "Christian Brothers Get Nailed." Father Walter "got all excited" about the IRS ending the abbey's tax exempt status, and so became even more cautious about the abbey's role in advertising Saint John's Bread.[68] As Father Walter explained to Interstate Bakeries' Charles Regan in 1962,

> According to government regulations we are not allowed to become active and to spend our royalty income for advertising or promotion. We do send some post-cards . . . but this is a minimum operation and only done for experimental purposes. We do not think that the government officials would object to this kind of personalized direct appeal to customers since the amount of money is insignificant in relation to income, since we do all the work here personally including the production, addressing, and mailing of the cards. I know that people like you and Graham think I am over-cautious about sending royalty money back into the competitive market, but I have made a careful study of the income tax laws governing these operations and I do not want to jeopardize the good name and reputation which Saint John's now enjoys.[69]

Regan replied that any attorney that would give such advice "is not too bright" and "should go back to college and study law again," but he could not change Father Walter's opinion.[70] The program would continue as it had begun. Not only did the abbey refuse to step up its advertising efforts in order to reverse declining sales, but Father Walter's concerns even caused him to quit hiring non-monastic personnel to address his postcards.

In summary, by late 1963, the bread program had reached a critical point. On the positive side, the abbey had received a total of $647,011 in royalties, and even at the reduced 1963 levels of $45,000 per year, Johnnie Bread made a significant contribution.[71] On the other hand, sales showed no sign of halting their downward plunge, and the strong network of franchises that had existed was shrinking rapidly. If the trend continued, it appeared that Johnnie Bread would soon disappear except in the Minnesota market, where loyal alumni sustained the demand. In short, it looked like Johnnie Bread was following the classic specialty bread pattern of initial success and slow decline. The only way to avoid this fate was to embark on a massive public relations campaign, but the means of doing so seemed remote. The remaining franchisees were not willing to invest more in a marginal product, and Father Walter was convinced that greater efforts by the abbey might generate very serious problems with the IRS. In this situation, needing a savior, Saint John's replaced its long-time mix supplier.

Notes

1. Of the six largest Standard Metropolitan Statistical areas east of the Alleghenies (New York City, Philadelphia, Boston, Washington, D.C., Baltimore, and Patterson-Clifton-Passaic), only Baltimore had a functioning franchise. US Bureau of the Census, *Statistical Abstract of the United States*, Washington: Government Printing Office, 1961, pp. 15-20.
2. "Saint John's Bread" (no date), ends December 1960, Abbey Archives, 320, Bread Contracts.
3. Interview with Father Florian Muggli, July 6, 1995.
4. Interview with Father Florian Muggli, July 6, 1995.
5. Virgil Michel, "Critique of Capitalism," in Robert Spaeth, editor, *The Social Question: Essays on Capitalism and Christianity by Father Virgil Michel, OSB*, Collegeville: Saint John's University, 1987, p. 32; Interview with Father Florian Muggli, July 6, 1995.
6. Interview with Father Florian Muggli, July 6, 1995.
7. Richard Walsh and Bert Evans, *Economics of Change in Market Structure, Conduct, and Performance in the Baking Industry*, Lincoln: University of Nebraska Press, 1963, p. 38.
8. Heegaard to Reger, April 27, 1959, Abbey Archives, 319, Peavey. QBA may even have been a more active detriment. Heegaard of Russell-Miller asserted that his company had "excellent connections" with some of the grocery chains, but suggested against using them because this would upset QBA.
9. Meyn to Hughes, February 11, 1960, Abbey Archives, 317, Interstate.
10. Interview with Father Florian Muggli, July 6, 1995.
11. Interstate took over Chicago some time in December 1959. At the peak, Interstate produced Johnnie Bread at thirty-two locations. Fourteen of these were in California. "Franchise and Specialty Breads," November 30, 1963, Abbey Archives, 317, Interstate.
12. The number of such in-store bakeries almost doubled between 1947 and 1958. Walsh and Evans, *Economics of Change*, p. 10.
13. Walsh and Evans, *Economics of Change*, p. 103.
14. Walsh and Evans, *Economics of Change*, p. 62.

15. Reger to Regan, January 20, 1960, Abbey Archives, 315, Interstate Bakeries.

16. Walsh and Evans, *Economics of Change*, p. 17, 102-106. See also comment that Washington is "largely dominated" by the large wholesalers and in-store bakeries. Heegard to Reger, April 27, 1959, Abbey Archives, 319, Peavey.

17. The four largest baking companies accounted for approximately 40 to 45 percent of the total value across the South. Only the Mountain states, with a 55 to 60 percent range was higher. The Midwest fell in the 30 percent range, with both coasts lower. Evans and Walsh, *Economics of Change*, p. 19. "QBA Members" (no date), Abbey Archives, 314, QBA.

18. These calculations don't include five QBA bakeries in the upper midwest that had already begun production. Based on data in Soukup to Rap-in-Wax, February 20, 1959, Abbey Archives, 319, Peavey, and "Analysis of Saint John's Mix Deliveries," August 24, 1960, Abbey Archives, 316, Bread Statistics.

19. Vanderpool to Baumann, March 10, 1960, and Baumann to Reger, May 11, 1960, Abbey Archives, 316, Saint John's Bread 1960. For evidence of the latter's earlier interest in Johnnie Bread, see Reger to Baird, approximately October 1959, Abbey Archives, 318, Bread File.

20. Reger to Baumann, May 16, 1960, Abbey Archives, 316, Saint John's Bread 1960.

21. Baumann to Reger, September 19, 1962, Abbey Archives, 315, QBA.

22. "Bread Statistics," December 1960, Abbey Archives, 316, Bread Statistics.

23. Saint John's Bread (no date), Abbey Archives, 316, Bread Statistics.

24. Calendar year 1959 sales were 96,264 sacks; 1960 sales were 89,058 sacks (no date). Abbey Archives, 316, Bread Statistics.

25. Saint John's Bread (no date), Abbey Archives, 316, Bread Statistics.

26. Jaeger, Lowenberg, Perfection, Stroehmans, Sweetheart, Jacobsen's, Merchants, and Reymond. Saint John's Bread (no date), and Analysis of Saint John's Mix Deliveries, August 24, 1960, Abbey Archives, 316, Bread Statistics.

27. Saint John's Bread (no date), and Analysis of Saint John's Mix Deliveries, August 24, 1960, Abbey Archives, 316, Bread Statistics.

28. 1961 sales were 56,816 sacks (no date); 1962 sales were 34,828 sacks; 1963 sales were 25,705 sacks. Abbey Archives, 316, Bread Statistics.

29. "Peavey Company - Comparative Deliveries," January 1964, Abbey Archives, 319, Peavey.

30. Franchise and Specialty Breads, November 30, 1963, Abbey Archives, 317, Interstate.

31. Reger to Baumann, June 7, 1962, Abbey Archives, 315, QBA.

32. "Alumni Chapters Begin Campaign to Aid Saint John's Bread Sales," *Off Campus Record*, April 1962, p. 11. Father Walter also tried to get alumni in areas where Johnnie Bread was available to pressure local grocers to carry it. See Back Cover, *Off Campus Record*, June 1961.

33. Hueter to Reger, June 14, 1962, and Reger to Hueter, June 22, 1962, Abbey Archives, 315, Interstate Bakeries.

34. Reger to Sullivan, September 15, 1960, Abbey Archives, 314, Betty Sullivan.

35. Baumann to Reger, September 19, 1962, Abbey Archives, 315, QBA.

36. Baumann to Reger, September 19, 1962.

37. The cost for Saint John's Dark was $0.1537 versus $0.0985 for Hollywood. The wholesale price for each was $0.24. "Comparison between Hollywood and Saint John's," April 11, 1960, Abbey Archives, 314, Rap-in-Wax.

38. Contract between Trappist Abbey of the Genesee and International Milling, March 11, 1960, Abbey Archives, 319, Contracts. Norm Groth indicated that in the 1990s, royalties on food products generally ranged from three to ten percent, so the fifteen to sixteen percent Saint John's received was "a pretty sizable royalty." Interview with Norm Groth, August 15, 1996.

39. Survey covers January 1958 to October 1960. Continuing Home Audit, Abbey Archives, 314, QBA 1959.

40. Saint John's Bread, December 1960, Abbey Archives, 320, Bread Contracts.

41. Saint John's Bread, December 1960, Abbey Archives, 320, Bread Contracts; "Peavey Company - Comparative Deliveries," January 1964, Abbey Archives, 319, Peavey.

42. Interview with Abbot Baldwin Dworschak, June 27, 1995.

43. William McGuire, quoted on "Comments and Quotes on the Reception of Saint John's Bread," Abbey Archives, 316, Batten, Barton, Durnstine, Osborne. Abbot Baldwin and Father Florian both commented that loaves produced from the mix were less coarse than the original. Interview with Abbot Baldwin Dworschak, June 27, 1995, and with Father Florian Muggli, July 6, 1995.

44. Vaughn to Reger, March 24, 1960, Abbey Archives, 315, International Milling.

45. Telephone interview with Tom Juettner, June 21, 1995; See also comment that "many alumni and friends have seemed to prefer the original," untitled clipping (no date), 318, Bread File.

46. See for example, Reger to Baumann, June 7, 1962, Abbey Archives, 315, QBA.

47. "Saint John's Bread" (no date), Abbey Archives, 320, Bread Contracts; "Saint John's Bread," December 1961, Abbey Archives, 316, Bread Statistics.

48. Heegaard to Reger, February 12, 1964, Abbey Archives, 319, Peavey Company.

49. General Comments and Suggestions (Graf's reply to Father Walter's letter of November 11, 1958), Abbey Archives, 314, QBA 1958.

50. "Detail of Services" (no date), Abbey Archives, 314, QBA 1958; Nicolait to Reger, February 26, 1959, Abbey Archives, 314, QBA 1959.

51. For evidence of overlap, see Sittard to Reger, November 22, 1959, Abbey Archives, 320, Herm Sittard; Reger to Regan, January 20, 1960, Abbey Archives, 315, Interstate Bakeries.

52. Sittard to Reger, Summary of projects to date, August 1963, Abbey Archives, 320, Herm Sittard.

53. Nolan to Reger, January 21, 1966, Abbey Archives, 314, Pillsbury Company; Shostrom to Williams, November 23, 1966, Abbey Archives, 320, Herm Sittard.

54. Reger to Baumann, June 7, 1962, Abbey Archives, 315, QBA.

55. Reger to Regan, January 20, 1960, Abbey Archives, 315, Interstate Bakeries.

56. Regan to Reger, June 17, 1963, Abbey Archives, 316, Interstate Bakeries.

57. Hueter to Reger, June 14, 1962, Abbey Archives, 315, Interstate Bakeries.

58. Reger to Hueter, June 22, 1962, Abbey Archives, 315, Interstate Bakeries.

59. This level of support came only in the early period, and for Abbey franchises. For example, of $7,924 in advertising services billed to McGuire's Lakeland Bakery before December 1959, $1,167 went to the Abbey and the rest to Stockinger. Account sheet for Lakeland Bakeries, Abbey Archives, 317, SJB Financial Data.

60. It is likely that Adrian's concern was prompted by controversy over a 1958 IRS regulation that apparently expanded tax exemptions for religious orders. "Tax Ruling Opposed," *New York Times*, July 18, 1958, p. 44.

61. Maun to Hughes, September 18, 1958, Abbey Archives, 320, Income-Expenses.

62. "Kennedy Praised," *New York Times*, January 3, 1960, p. 44.

63. Juettner to Reger, August 26, 1960, Abbey Archives, 320, Trademark.

64. Reger to Juettner, August 29, 1960, Abbey Archives, 320, Trademark.

65. Interview with Father Florian Muggli, July 6, 1995.

66. Reger to Arno, February 5, 1963, University Archives, 1605:5, Bread SJU.

67. "Tax Case Resolved," *New York Times*, December 2, 1961, p. 12.

68. Interview with Father Gervase Soukup, July 7, 1995.

69. Reger to Regan, February 14, 1962, Abbey Archives, 317, Interstate Bakeries.

70. Regan to Reger, June 17, 1963, Abbey Archives, 316, Interstate Bakeries.

71. Royalty total from Heegaard to Reger, February 12, 1964, Abbey Archives, 319, Peavey Company.

Chapter Five

The Doughboy to the Rescue?

The relationship between Saint John's and Russell-Miller Milling was a deep one, rooted in the abbey's gratitude to the company for its help in developing the mix, and in the mutual affection between Father Walter and Russell-Miller's Dr. Betty Sullivan. Changes following the Peavey Company's absorption of Russell-Miller removed Dr. Sullivan from a direct connection with Saint John's, but the amicable spirit remained until the backwash from declining sales began to erode the foundations.

Russell-Miller had initially agreed to supply the mix to bakers essentially at cost, charging $9.10 per hundred-pound sack. The expectation, soon realized, was that as volume increased, economies of scale in production would allow the company to achieve reasonable profits. In this situation, Russell-Miller/Peavey was willing to maintain the original price despite some increases in costs until the mix sales began to fall. As early as June 1962, Peavey's William Heegaard wrote Father Walter, complaining that higher material costs justified a sixty cents per sack increase, and pointing out that the decline in sales raised production costs per unit as well. Since raising the price sharply might cause more bakers to drop Johnnie Bread, Heegaard suggested that the abbey cut its royalty by twenty cents per sack.[1] Father Walter agreed to discussions but resolutely defended the Saint John's royalty, so Peavey ultimately decided to continue with a declining profit margin.

The continued downward trend in sales, plus higher wheat and labor costs, brought Heegaard back to the same issue again eighteen months later. In a much more assertive tone in early 1964, he informed Father Walter that his company needed at least fifty cents a sack more if it was to continue. Heegaard urged the abbey to accept the fifty-cents-per-sack cut in its royalties.[2]

Father Walter's immediate response is not recorded, but one can well guess given the sharp decline in revenues already experienced. Rather than accept Heegaard's analysis, Father Walter reached out to alternative sources for countervailing information. George Kolb of the Belgrade Flour Mill refuted Peavey's evidence that higher wheat prices justified a fifty cent increase, while contacts at Interstate Bakeries reported that they expected some price increase, and that even if it were as high as fifty cents, they "would be willing to absorb it rather than have Saint John's reduce its royalty income."[3] Thus armed, Father Walter stood firm, effectively forestalling a price increase yet again.

Father Walter was clearly unhappy with what he regarded as an effort to shore up Peavey's profits at Saint John's expense, but this in itself still wasn't sufficient grounds for divorce. The critical element for those running the Saint John's program was the realization that the pattern of rapidly falling sales could not be reversed without additional marketing strength. This awareness made them very willing to listen when the Pillsbury Company came calling during the summer of 1964.[4] Even so, Father Walter was reluctant to move. While being courted by Pillsbury, Father Walter wrote an imploring letter to his old friend at Peavey, Dr. Betty Sullivan, assuring her that "if Peavey had given or could now give convincing evidence that it can and will supply a marketing and merchandising program comparable to the one being offered by Pillsbury, our committee would remain with Peavey."[5] Lacking Pillsbury's resources, however, Peavey threw in the towel, failing even to accept Father Walter's offer of a final meeting.[6] By November 1964, Pillsbury had taken over officially as the new supplier of the Saint John's mix. The change, as Father Florian Muggli acknowledged, was painful given Peavey's prior help and the "special obligation to Betty," but it was nevertheless "a business judgement" that had to be made.[7]

The Pillsbury Contract

While the Pillsbury contract kept the ingredients price stable and retained the traditional $1.50 per sack royalty for Saint John's, there were two key changes.[8] First, the old requirement that bakers prove that they had spent at least $1.50 per sack on advertising was replaced by a direct charge of $1.40 included in the price of each bag of the mix. This money went to an advertising fund controlled by Pillsbury, thus effectively centralizing the promotional effort.[9] Franchisees could still launch their own efforts, but, in return for the $1.40 advertising charge, Pillsbury offered bakers scripts, ad mats, art work, and contest ideas, all for "free."[10] Any postcard campaigns from Father Walter's office were also charged to this account. In a further effort to achieve better coordination, Pillsbury and Saint John's also signed a separate, temporary agreement with Tom Rowan (SJU '36), a food broker. For a small part of the price of each sack, Rowan promised to oversee current contracts, seek out new franchisees, oversee advertising, monitor accounts and in general act as the coordinating agent for the program.[11]

Despite his sorrow about leaving Dr. Betty Sullivan and the disruption of the transition, the move to Pillsbury must have looked like a godsend to Father Walter and others involved in the bread program. Rowan's presence not only centralized responsibilities that had previously been divided between the abbey, QBA, Interstate Bakeries, Peavey, and others, but also provided a professional to search out new markets and reduced the need for a direct Saint John's role. Furthermore, it seemed safe to assume that the $1.40 per sack advertising fee would result in a net increase in impact under Pillsbury's control. After all, as the company pointed out during its courtship of Father Walter, they offered not just coordination and expertise, but also access "on a national basis with leading chains, supermarkets, independent wholesale as well as retail bakery accounts."[12] Furthermore, Pillsbury promised to use its experienced personnel, including the National Sales Manager of the Bakery Products Division, to launch Saint John's Bread in key markets such as Chicago, Cincinnati, St. Louis, and Denver.[13] It was just the cure for a specialty bread that had lost visibility and whose market had shrunk to a few isolated locations.

Frozen Dough

For Father Walter, the icing on the Pillsbury cake must have been its commitment to one of his pet projects, the development of a frozen dough that would allow home baking of Johnnie Bread. Ever since 1958, Father Walter had been looking for ways to expand the product line. Initially he had focused on getting bakers to use the mix to produce hot dog and hamburger buns. Despite his own enthusiasm, Father Walter at least temporarily accepted the argument that expensive buns wouldn't sell, replying "certainly this is true as long as people are apparently happy with the cheap ones they are now buying with which to convey wieners and hamburgers to their gruelling lips."[14] Another idea was to provide a mix that could be prepared at home; experiments in Peg Gagliardi's kitchen, however, produced only "bricks."[15] Frozen dough for home baking seemed the next logical option. Aside from convenience, it would allow housewives to "achieve a product which practically duplicates the one that comes from our abbey kitchens" and avoid the problems of improper commercial baking. Ever the optimist, Father Walter was certain that if a quality frozen dough were put on the market, it would "expand our sales by at least fifty percent in a very short time."[16]

Pursuing this dream, Father Walter began early in 1963 to lobby Peavey for a frozen dough. After some delay, the manufacturer's Bakery Sales and Service Department agreed to experiment but took no action.[17] Frustrated, Father Walter sought other help, appealing to Ray Thelen, an acquaintance who was the technical director of Pillsbury's Bakery Products Division.[18] In October 1963, Thelen responded: "The frozen dough idea you and I talked about on several occasions should be exploited. Our company research group hasn't had an opportunity to spend developmental time on the project as yet; however, should you find a baker interested in producing it, I'm sure we could put him in business in a relatively short time."[19] Encouraged, Father Walter quickly got the Red Owl stores in the Twin Cities to agree to market a frozen dough, but Peavey continued to put off development.[20]

Pillsbury played on Father Walter's commitment to the frozen dough adroitly during negotiations, offering "to put our test bakery, as well as research and development laboratory, to work on this project at once."[21] Once the contract was signed, Pillsbury upheld its promise, but the project proved more difficult than Thelen had suggested. First, since the standard mix proved unsuitable for the frozen product, a new formula had to be developed.[22] That problem had been solved by March 1965, but delays continued because Pillsbury's researchers couldn't find a way to insure the desired frozen shelf life of twelve months.[23] Father Walter finally got his frozen dough on the market in early 1966, joyously announcing to alumni that "now housewives can bake it themselves like the abbey does, on the hearth (cookie sheet) in their own kitchen ovens!"[24] Unfortunately, this product continued to experience problems with quality and shelf life to the extent that some observers thought it hurt the overall image of Saint John's Bread.[25] Sales reached a peak of 659 bags of mix in fiscal year 1967, but then fell rapidly to zero by 1970.[26]

Hanging on with Pillsbury

The "slow rise" of the frozen bread dough program mirrored the trajectory of the early Pillsbury effort in general. Rather than an immediate revival, sales of the famous loaf continued to decline in late 1964 and throughout 1965. Sales for the year ending May 31, 1966, were only 10,052 sacks, or one-third of what they had been in the last full year with Peavey.[27] The monthly reports from Interstate Bakeries told the tale in stark and painful clarity. By late 1963, the number of Interstate-associated bakeries producing Johnnie Bread had shrunk to an even dozen, but the West Coast plants were still doing well.[28] This, too, would turn sour in 1964 and 1965. Month after month, Father Walter neatly filed Interstate Bakeries' reports with their news of fewer plants and

Although the commercial sales of Johnnie Bread had declined sharply by the mid-1960s, the famous loaf remained a hot item on campus. Clubs, such as the Pre-Med Society in this photo, sold bread at Homecoming and other alumni-attended events to raise money for their activities. (Photo courtesy of Saint John's University Archives)

declining sales. By November 1965, however, he no longer had the stomach for such orderliness; the last monthly statement was not unfolded and filed but rather replaced in its envelope and tossed in with other correspondence. The news was enough to make anyone despair. In November 1965, the last Interstate bakery making Johnnie Bread sold only twenty-seven white loaves.[29]

In an effort to jump start a program that increasingly looked like a candidate for last rites, Pillsbury launched a new marketing ploy. After months of planning, in May 1966, the world was introduced to the new symbol for the famous loaf: "Brother John," a round, tonsured and sandaled monk wearing a Franciscan habit.[30] (Father Walter received lots of ribbing about the incorrect attire from his confreres, to which he replied, "That's what people think monks look like," and, "We're not going to be so selfish anyway."[31]) With Brother John, the old Metten to Minnesota, and *Schwarzbrot*, the commer-

In 1966, Pillsbury introduced the new "Brother John" character as part of an advertising campaign to revive Johnnie Bread sales. The postcard approach was continued, except that the personal note from Father Walter on the reverse side was now frequently transformed into a standardized printed version shown here. Some deluxe versions of this postcard were printed in a folded-over book format, with Pillsbury's romanticized story of Brother John and the transmission of the recipe from Metten to Minnesota printed on the inside. (Photo courtesy of Saint John's Abbey Archives)

90

Pillsbury publicists followed their own stereotypes about monastic profiles in choosing this actor to represent "Brother John." Father Walter endured substantial teasing within the monastery for using a man in a Franciscan habit to promote Benedictine bread. He responded to his tormentors by pointing out that the actor fit "what people think monks look like," and gently chiding them not to be "so selfish" as to insist on proper Benedictine attire. (Photo courtesy of Saint John's University Archives)

cial sales story was personalized. The monk was portrayed as sad when nuns "newly arrived from France" took over the kitchen and forced him to "hang up his well-floured apron." He soon "was able to chuckle and smile again," for he found that "Saint John's Bread baked by the nuns tasted as good as ever, and its fame with the monks and Saint John's University students had not been harmed at all." After tracing other changes, the saga concluded, "Brother John's jolly face would beam again if he knew that today Saint John's Bread is available to millions of people. Full bodied in both the DARK, rough-grain loaf and a companion WHITE loaf, Saint John's Bread is baked today at franchised bakers throughout the country."[32]

Along with the introduction of Brother John in 1966, Pillsbury also launched a more significant change in marketing strategy. Pillsbury's initial preference had been to pursue one of the national bakers —Interstate Bakeries, American, or Continental Baking—and convince them to take Johnnie Bread nation wide.[33] Given that Interstate Bakeries would watch its sales decline to zero in 1965, it isn't surprising that even "a full scale presentation" was insufficient to get any of the big three to invest the significant resources necessary for such a campaign.[34] Moving to the second option, Pillsbury's strategists sought to restore sales through a renewed appeal to the same independent wholesale bakers who had formed the core of the program in the glory years.[35] A few were attracted, probably by the prospect of help from Pillsbury's marketing resources, but, on the whole, the results were disappointing.[36] Finally, in the spring of 1966, Pillsbury's executives decided to make supermarket chains, including those with in-store bakeries, the prime focus of their blandishments.

Given their predilection for house brands, marketing to the supermarket chains promised to be a tough nut to crack, but Pillsbury's decision made sense in terms of growth potential. Between 1965 and 1967, wholesale bakery sales increased four percent, while supermarket bakeries saw a 7.1 percent gain. These trends were magnified in the critical specialty bread arena, where the 3.8 percent increase for wholesale bakeries was dwarfed by the 8.2 percent figure for supermarkets.[37]

As hoped, some supermarket chains did sign on. By early 1967, Johnnie Bread was available in fifty Ralph's stores in Southern California, the Kings Sooper chain in Denver, a few subsidiaries of the National Tea Company, and in some Safeway stores.[38] Every success filled Father Walter with renewed optimism, but the results were far below what he and his Pillsbury associates hoped. For example, Pillsbury National Sales Manager Robert Dwyer had predicted that all of the 256 Safeways in the West would pick up the mix.[39] Instead, the total was less than a dozen, mostly in the San Francisco Bay Area, and their sales were low; in fiscal year 1967, the abbey kitchens used more bags of mix than did all the Safeway outlets combined.[40]

While the results didn't meet expectations, Pillsbury's efforts did enable the famous loaf to continue in the marketplace for a little while longer. Brother John and the new marketing strategies halted the free fall of sales experienced between 1963 and 1965, and even brought a slight rebound. Total sales for fiscal year 1967 were a little over one percent higher than in fiscal year 1966, with the abbey's monthly royalties hitting a Pillsbury peak of $2,007 in August 1966.[41] This "peak," however, looked more like a small hummock when measured against the $20,000 per month royalties from the glory days of late 1959. Unfortunately, not even this level could be sustained; by 1969, a monthly royalty check of over $1,000 had become exceptional.[42]

Not only did overall sales decline as the 1960s wore on, but the traditional dark loaf became an increasingly insignificant part of the equation. Through 1962, the wheat loaf accounted for fifty-eight percent of total sales. Over the next several years, its share slowly dropped, until, by 1966, Dr. Sullivan's white companion loaf outproduced the classic version by a two to one margin. Finally bottoming out with thirty percent of the sales in 1969, the favorite loaf of Collegeville never regained its status in the commercial world as the foremost Johnnie Bread.[43] While Saint John's white bread certainly had more substance than its mass market rivals, the dark loaf's decline must have added to Father Walter's disappointment for its fall made it clear that he would not realize his hope to get the nation to "eat nourishing bread again."[44]

Why the Resuscitation Failed

Pillsbury was unable to restore either version of Johnnie Bread as a significant source of income for Saint John's for several reasons. Above all, the changing nature of the marketplace made success for an independent specialty bread increasingly difficult. The consolidation of the wholesale bread market and the growth of supermarkets with their own house brands meant that products like Johnnie Bread faced a David versus Goliath situation. Pillsbury's contacts, while impressive, weren't any substitute for divine intervention, so the outcome was predictable. Even the best bread can't win customers if it isn't given shelf space. Furthermore, it may have been that Pillsbury's assistance wasn't quite what Father Walter had expected. Tom LeNeau, who worked for Pillsbury in the early 1960s, asserts that since the commission rate that Pillsbury sales agents got for Johnnie Bread was comparatively low, they had less incentive to push the product hard. When LeNeau suggested finding ways to resolve this, Father Walter's response was that the sales force should work hard regardless because it was their job to sell.[45]

The second major problem was that while the move to Pillsbury improved the coordination of advertising, it failed to solve the more fundamental problem of adequate resources. Once the appeal to the major baking companies failed, the bread program was once again dependent on monies generated by the sale of the mix. While the Pillsbury structure meant that these funds would be used in a more efficient manner than before, they still weren't sufficient for a massive campaign since Pillsbury collected slightly less per bag for advertising than bakers had been required to spend earlier. Furthermore, the new arrangements also failed to address the inherent problems in a system that provided more money for advertising only as the product succeeded.

Pillsbury executives recognized these problems from the beginning but evidently didn't see their company as the source of a solution.[46] Instead, like others before, Bakery Products Division Manager Norman Groth asked Saint John's to contribute more to advertising. With his prize frozen bread effort hanging in the balance, Father Walter made a concession. Agreeing that "the advertising and promotional factor in the program was not adequate to effectively introduce fresh or *frozen bread*"(emphasis added), he agreed to cut the abbey's royalty by fifty cents for a few months "if needed."[47] The reduction, however, applied only to the embryonic frozen dough program, so its impact was minimal.[48] While Groth was undoubtedly disappointed with the result, he didn't give up hope, continuing to insist that Saint John's do more. When a new effort in Miami was proposed, he argued for a delay "until the abbey is able to provide some additional marketing and sales guidance . . ." because "we do not want the same pattern to develop here as is developing in Los Angeles, Seattle, and Denver."[49] More specifically, what Groth had in mind was hiring a new third party to replace Tom Rowan, who evidently was no longer in the picture. This new "professional bread merchandiser" would "be completely isolated on the promotion of the Saint John's bread product and would eat, sleep, and continually think of ways that they could sell more Saint John's bread.[50] Unlike Rowan or the Pillsbury sales agents who were paid on a commission basis from mix sales, Groth envisioned a person who would be paid directly by Saint John's.[51]

Business office approval of such a tax on dwindling bread revenues was highly unlikely anyway, but the issue didn't even get that far since Father Walter continued to insist that "Saint John's could be in real trouble with the federal government if it used its bread income for intense promotional efforts."[52] Thus limited, Father Walter fell back on his old stand-by, firing off postcards at every opportunity. For example, when the Safeway stores in Washington, D.C., began to sell Johnnie Bread in 1968, he asked the chain for the addresses of its stores so that he could "notify our Saint John's alumni (including Senator [Eugene] McCarthy) and hundreds of Minnesota friends in Washington."[53] Buoyed by his faith in the appeal of the famous loaf, Father Walter continued to hope that activating alumni and friends would insure shelf space and sales.

The End of Father Walter's Efforts

Unfortunately, as the 1960s continued, even these personal promotional efforts by Father Walter were curtailed by his declining health. Although Abbot Baldwin would later characterize Father Walter as "this frail monk and priest who was plagued with illness all his life," those who observed him in the 1960s continued to marvel at his energy.[54] For example, early in the decade, Father Walter astounded a recent graduate by suggesting and completing a two block run in the rain from their parking place to a meeting in Minneapolis.[55] The stop signs began to go up, however, in 1966 when Father Walter suffered a heart attack just weeks short of his seventy-second birthday. This attack not only kept him from going to the West Coast to assist with promotions there but required that he give up all activity at home for several weeks.[56] By August 1966, Father Walter reported that he was "in reasonably good health again" but acknowledged that he had "to pace it more slowly."[57] A little over two years later, he was back in the Saint Cloud hospital, and apparently never regained full health.[58] Without Father Walter's driving energy behind it, Johnnie Bread lost one of the few promotional advantages that it still possessed.

As the 1960s continued, Father Walter realized that "when you are dealing with the business world . . . things are out of your control no matter how good the quality may be of a product or bread."[59] By 1967, he was willing to acknowledge that the "new route" taken with Pillsbury "has proved very disappointing" and occasionally contemplated surrender. When Tom Juettner asked why he hadn't returned an application for renewal of a state trademark, Father Walter replied, "The reason for the non-response has been, at least in part,

95

Father Walter was disappointed that bread sales didn't provide a permanent endowment, but the program had helped with many dramatic changes on campus. By 1967, when this photo was taken, the Breuer-designed Science Hall, Alcuin Library, and the abbey church (on right) were in use. While the physical changes were spectacular, they told only part of the story. Saint John's had grown to almost 1,500 students, while the number of monks teaching them declined; in 1967, lay people made up forty percent of the faculty. A few miles down the road in Saint Joseph, enrollment at the College of Saint Benedict was nearly 500 women, and the college was entering a period of rapid expansion that would soon make it as large as Saint John's. The schools had begun the first tentative efforts at academic cooperation. (Photo courtesy of Saint John's Abbey Archives)

that the Saint John's bread sales have declined to the point where I wonder whether I shouldn't give up."[60] Instead of quitting, however, Father Walter continued to cast about for ways to revive sales. In 1968, for example, he gathered the names of several potential candidates for a promotional middleman position and even agreed that Brownberry Bread and other specialty producers be approached to gauge their interest in adding Johnnie Bread to their product lines.[61] On a smaller scale, he and Tom LeNeau also tried to find a way to have the famous loaf available for sale to travelers in the Minneapolis-Saint Paul airport.[62] While these initiatives came to naught, Father Walter was "still hopeful" until his death.[63]

When Father Walter died on January 18, 1971, the bread program had reached a very low ebb. Zinsmaster Bakeries, with its advertising supplemented by loyal alumni in the Twin Cities and Duluth, was a lonely flagship. Indeed, at the time of Father Walter's death, the Twin Cities firm accounted for seventy-five percent of the mix used outside the abbey. While the 4,840 sacks it consumed that year was only one-third of its 1959 figure, the volume seemed to be holding steady. Elsewhere the picture was bleak. Of the various supermarket chains recruited under Pillsbury, four sites remained, but they accounted for a total sales of only 121 sacks. Worse yet, once again alumni had little chance of enjoying the famous loaf unless they lived in Minnesota. Only one of the five bakers still using more than seventy-five sacks of mix per year was outside the state. The benefit to the abbey was also slipping away, as overall royalties averaged barely over $800 per month in fiscal year 1971.[64]

Although his good friend Abbot Baldwin characterized Father Walter as a "frail monk," he showed great stamina until a heart attack slowed him in 1966. He was able to resume some of his duties soon afterward but suffered a second attack in late 1968, from which he never really recovered. When the monks gathered for their annual Christmas party in 1970, Abbot Baldwin convinced the Saint Cloud Hospital to release Father Walter for the evening. When it was time for Father Walter to return to the hospital, the monks broke into a spontaneous round of "For He's a Jolly Good Fellow," thus expressing "in this secular way the gratitude of fifty years of monks. Tears such as he had never shed rolled down Walter's cheeks and, embarrassed, he signed Brother Raphael to wheel him from the hall. Monk by monk pressed his hand or his shoulder as the chair moved to the door." Father Walter died on January 18, 1971 at the age of seventy-six, about nine months after this photo was taken. (Photo courtesy of Saint John's Abbey Archives)

While Father Walter was no doubt disappointed that he hadn't found a way to create the permanent "endowment" that he had sought, his efforts had led to some very significant gains. During his tenure, Saint John's had gained $562,878 in net income on royalties of approximately $600,000.[65] Furthermore, as many have pointed out, the bread program was also a success in that it spurred alumni loyalty and got "the Saint John's name known around the country."[66] Finally, the commercial sales of the famous loaf exposed many Americans to a quality bread and, thereby, may have helped to shift the nation's taste. Much of the credit must go to Father Walter's energy, enthusiasm, and the friends that he made for Saint John's as he sought to spread the word on the famous loaf.

Notes

1. Heegaard to Reger, June 25, 1962, Abbey Archives, 319, Peavey.

2. Heegaard to Reger, February 12, 1964, Abbey Archives, 319, Peavey Company.

3. Reger to Kolb, July 15, 1964, Abbey Archives, 319, Peavey.

4. It is unclear who initiated this first contact. Father Walter had already contacted Ray Thelen of Pillsbury about a frozen dough in 1963 (see subsequent section of text). Tom LeNeau said that he believed that the gregarious, Catholic, and Saint Cloud-raised Thelen had met Father Walter at a convention, and that this led to the frozen dough discussion. Thelen doesn't remember any contact on the frozen dough but only being sent by Pillsbury to see Father Walter about reformulating the mix in 1964. Norm Groth believes that the initiative for the Pillsbury bid to become the mix supplier came from Robert Dwyer, a Pillsbury executive who was "a very active Catholic." According to Groth, Dwyer heard of the tensions with Peavey through industry gossip and wanted to help Saint John's. Unfortunately Robert Dwyer died before the authors began this project. Interview with Tom LeNeau, July 22, 1996; Interview with Ray Thelen, August 21, 1996; Interview with Norm Groth, August 15, 1996.

5. Reger to Sullivan, September 9, 1964, Abbey Archives, 314, Betty Sullivan.

6. Dr. Betty Sullivan acknowledged in 1996 that Pillsbury enjoyed a substantial marketing advantage over her company. Interview with Dr. Betty Sullivan, August 26, 1996.

7. Muggli to Heegaard, September 29, 1964, Abbey Archives, 319, Contracts.

8. Pillsbury raised the price per sack but included transportation. The cost of ingredients per loaf in 1960 was $0.078. The projected cost four years later under Pillsbury was $0.80. "Comparison between Hollywood and Saint John's," April 11, 1960, Abbey Archives, 314, Rap-in-Wax; "Profit, Price, Policy" (no date), Abbey Archives, 318, Saint John's Bread - Total Program.

9. "Profit, Price, Policy" (no date), Abbey Archives, 318, Saint John's Bread - Total Program.

10. "Services" (no date), Abbey Archives, 318, Saint John's Bread - Total Program.

11. Rowan to Reger, September 9, 1964, and Groth memo, November 9, 1964, Abbey Archives, 316, Pillsbury.

12. Saint John's Bread Program by Robert Dwyer, August 31, 1964, Abbey Archives, 314, Pillsbury.

13. Dwyer to Reger, September 2, 1964, Abbey Archives, 314, Pillsbury Company.

14. Reger to Sittard, September 16, 1960, Abbey Archives, 320, Sittard. Hamburger buns weren't sold until 1970. Coolidge to Sales Personnel, April 13, 1970, Abbey Archives, 316, Pillsbury.

15. Interview with Peg Gagliardi, November 27, 1996.

16. Reger to Heegaard, Abbey Archives, March 19, 1964, 319, Peavey.

17. Hubers to Muggli, December 20, 1963, Abbey Archives, 319, Peavey.

18. See note 4 above.

19. Thelen to Reger, October 2, 1963, Abbey Archives, 314, Pillsbury Correspondence.

20. Reger to Juettner, March 11, 1965, Abbey Archives, 320, Trademarks.

21. Saint John's Bread Program by Robert Dwyer, August 31, 1964, Abbey Archives, 314, Pillsbury.

22. Nolan to Groth, January 26, 1965, Abbey Archives, 316, Pillsbury.

23. Reger to Juettner, March 11, 1965.

24. Father Walter Reger, "We're In the Dough—Frozen That Is!" *Off Campus Record*, winter 1965, p. 7; Gaertner to Food Editor, February 2, 1966, Abbey Archives, 314, Pillsbury.

25. Moran to Mead, January 10, 1973, Abbey Archives, 316, Bread Statistics. One of the key problems in a frozen dough continues to be handling the yeast. See interviews with Dr. Betty Sullivan, August 26, 1996, and Ray Thelen, August 21, 1996.

26. Frozen bread is product code 6956. "Saint John's Bread Mixes," May 1967, Abbey Archives, 316, Pillsbury-Monthly Statements; "Saint John's Deliveries," May 1971, Abbey Archives, 318, Bread File.

27. In fiscal year 1963, 30,586 sacks were sold. Heegaard to Reger, February 12, 1964, Abbey Archives, 319, Peavey; "Saint John's Bread Mixes - May 1967," Abbey Archives, 316, Pillsbury - Monthly Statements.

28. "Gross Sales and Stale Units," November 30, 1963, Abbey Archives, 317, Interstate.

29. "Gross Sales and Stale Units," November 27, 1965.

30. "Pillsbury Saint John's Loaf," *Southwestern Miller,* May 10, 1966, Abbey Archives, 316, Batten, Barton, Durstine.

31. Interview with Father Florian Muggli, July 6, 1995.

32. "The Legend of Saint John's Bread" (no date), Abbey Archives, 315, Zinsmaster.

33. Nolan to Groth, January 26, 1965, Abbey Archives, 316, Pillsbury.

34. Dwyer to Reger, April 26, 1966, Abbey Archives, 314, Pillsbury Correspondence.

35. Nolan to Groth, January 26, 1965.

36. By April 1966, the Ruth Ashbrook Bakery of Seattle had placed an order, while a Portland bakery was close to an agreement and Schmidt's of Baltimore had "expressed an interest in taking on the bread again." Dwyer to Reger, April 26, 1966, Abbey Archives, 314, Pillsbury Correspondence.

37. Neil Alden, "Baking Trends," June 3, 1968, Abbey Archives, 320, Herm Sittard.

38. "Saint John's Bread Mixes - May 1967," Abbey Archives, 316, Pillsbury - Monthly Statements.

39. Dwyer to Reger, April 26, 1966, Abbey Archives, 314, Pillsbury Correspondence.

40. The abbey used 610 bags of mix versus a total of 607 bags delivered to eleven Safeway stores. "Saint John's Bread Mixes," May 1967, Abbey Archives, 316, Pillsbury - Monthly Statements.

41. This was highly unusual, since the next highest monthly totals were in the $1,200 to $1,300 range. Royalty Statement, August 1966, Abbey Archives, 316, Pillsbury.

42. Royalty Statements, 1969, Abbey Archives, 314, Pillsbury.

43. Saint John's Bread, Abbey Archives, 320, Bread Contracts; Saint John's Bread, December 1962, Abbey Archives, 316, Bread Statistics; Peavey Deliveries, Abbey Archives, 319, Peavey; Saint John's Bread Mix Deliveries, 1966-1971, Abbey Archives, 316, Pillsbury Monthly Statements.

44. Interview with Father Gordon Tavis, August 9, 1994.

45. Interview with Tom LeNeau, July 22, 1996. Norm Groth, the Manager of Pillsbury's Bakery Products Division believes that the sales staff promoted Johnnie Bread, but acknowledges that it was one product among many they sold, and furthermore that the regular Pillsbury products had a higher margin. Interview with Norm Groth, August 15, 1996.

46. Interview with Norm Groth, August 15, 1996; Nolan to Groth, January 26, 1965, Abbey Archives, 316, Pillsbury.

47. Nolan to Reger, August 5, 1965, Abbey Archives, 314, Pillsbury Correspondence.

48. Groth to Muggli, July 20, 1966, Abbey Archives, 314, Pillsbury Company.

49. Groth to Baier, October 28, 1966, Abbey Archives, 316, Batten, Barton, Durstine, and Osborn.

50. Interview with Norm Groth, August 15, 1996.

51. Groth to Muggli, July 20, 1966, Abbey Archives, 314, Pillsbury Company.

52. Reger to Hoffman, October 5, 1966, Abbey Archives, 316, Red Owl.

53. Reger to Safeway, July 10, 1968, Abbey Archives, 317, Safeway.
54. Death Notice for Father Walter Reger, January 18, 1971, Abbey Archives.
55. Interview with Lee Hanley, July 11, 1996.
56. Durenberger to Baier, May 13, 1966, Abbey Archives, 319, Contracts; Moran to Mead, January 10, 1973, Abbey Archives, 316, Bread Statistics.
57. Reger to Juettner, August 8, 1966, Abbey Archives, 320, Trademark.
58. Muggli to Juettner, December 19, 1968, Abbey Archives, 320, Trademarks.
59. Interview with Abbot Baldwin Dworschak, June 27, 1995.
60. Reger to Juettner, May 1, 1967.
61. The issue of who would pay for the middleman was not clarified. Hall to Reger, February 13, 1995, Abbey Archives, 314, Pillsbury Correspondence.
62. Interview with Tom LeNeau, July 22, 1996.
63. Telephone interview with Tom Juettner, June 21, 1995.
64. "Saint John's Deliveries," May 1971, Abbey Archives, 318, Bread File.
65. Net figures from Father Gervase Soukup and Saint John's Annual Audit Reports. The royalty figures are approximate because the author was unable to find a full accounting for 1963 and 1964 during the transition to Pillsbury.
66. Telephone interview with Tom Juettner, June 21, 1995; Interview with Abbot Baldwin Dworschak, June 27, 1995.

Chapter Six

New Initiatives and Old Results

Father Walter Reger's funeral marked just one of many transitions at Saint John's in 1971. Just months after Father Walter's death, his long time friend, Abbot Baldwin Dworschak, announced that he would give up the leadership position he had held for twenty years. The monastery soon elected Prior John Eidenschink as Abbot Baldwin's replacement. On the university side, Father Colman Barry also stepped down after seven years as president, giving way to fellow historian Father Michael Blecker. Father Colman, like Abbot Baldwin, had overseen many innovations, including the creation of the Center for Ecumenical and Cultural Research, the Hill Monastic Microfilm Library, and the first affiliate of Minnesota Public Radio.

Picking Up the Pieces

While the procedures for the transfer of power in the abbey and university were clear, Father Walter's death left the bread program an orphan without even any close family. The first person to try to come to the rescue was Tom LeNeau, who had left Pillsbury in 1966 to become financial manager of the Liturgical Press at Saint John's. LeNeau had often given Father Walter rides to Pillsbury when he was going to the Twin Cities on Liturgical Press business, and the two tried to arrange their schedule so they could "stick" someone from Pillsbury for "lunch at the Minneapolis Club if we were lucky."[1] Beyond the ensuing conversations, however, LeNeau had had no direct connection with the bread program. His experience with Pillsbury had convinced LeNeau that the famous loaf had already outlasted the limited life span of most specialty breads, but he saw no reason why Johnnie Bread couldn't continue to produce a small, but steady income from sales in the Upper Midwest. Stepping in after Father Walter's death, LeNeau realized that his first task was simply to find out what had been going on in what had become a one man operation.[3] Plaintively asking for information on Johnnie Bread outlets, LeNeau wrote Aaron Petersen of Zinsmaster Baking Company, "Father Walter probably knew all of this, but we are unable to locate this information. . . . "[4]

Although LeNeau was largely content to get the existing accounts in order, a second player, recently hired Food Service Director Jerry Mead, was "very interested in helping to get Saint John's Bread moving again on the commercial market."[5] A coffee salesman earlier in his career, Mead was "a real dynamo" who wasn't easily deterred by obstacles.[6] (Lacking funds to expose the original brick in the student refectory, Mead got students to volunteer their time to strip the over-layer of plaster in return for beer and late night snacks.[7]) Evidently figuring that selling bread was little different than pushing coffee beans, Mead believed that he could restore Johnnie Bread as a major revenue source. He began that effort in 1972, when he convinced the new owners of what had been Graham McGuire's Lakeland Bakery to resume commercial production of the famous loaf in Saint Cloud.[8]

While Mead played an important role, the key figure in the effort to resurrect the bread program was Father Gordon Tavis, who returned to Collegeville in the summer of 1972 after a year of management classes at the Massachusetts Institute of Technology. As the university's new Vice President for Administrative Services, Father Gordon's responsibilities included "auxiliary services," which gave him the opportunity to pursue a number of initiatives.[9] Believing that "the whole of the bread business has a good future," Father Gordon devoted some of his considerable energies to investigating the prospects.[10] He dug through the archives, contacted those still involved in the program, and even arranged a meeting to discuss the bread business with Stanley Anderson, whose Hillbilly Bread was

When Father Gordon Tavis, OSB, returned to Saint John's in 1972 after graduate training at the Massachusetts Institute of Technology, he was anxious to find ways to generate non-tuition revenue for the university. Believing that Johnnie Bread still had a commercial potential that could be translated into meaningful support for scholarships, he led the effort to resuscitate Father Walter's program. (Photo courtesy of Saint John's Abbey Archives)

the number one seller in the nation. As he told Anderson, he wanted to expand the Saint John's operation because "you might almost say that every dollar that we can produce is a dollar for scholarship funds."[11]

Although he was ready to take on the challenge, Father Gordon needed to clear one critical organizational hurdle. The bread program was administratively an abbey or corporate responsibility, rather than belonging to the university. Father Gervase Soukup, the abbey procurator (treasurer), shared Father Gordon's faith in Johnnie Bread's potential but didn't think that he could get support within the abbey to try to revive it. As a result, Father Gervase arranged to transfer the bread program to Father Gordon's university portfolio,

Jerry Mead (right) played a key role in the 1970s efforts to find a new commercial niche for the famous Collegeville loaf. With boundless enthusiasm and great sales ability, Jerry sought new opportunities with grocery chains and with institutions such as schools and hospitals. To lower costs, he also recruited new regional mix blenders who could supply local clients. (Photo courtesy of Jerry Mead) with Father Gordon agreeing to guarantee the abbey $12,000 net income per year.[12] As a result, from late 1972 on, it was Father Gordon who would make the critical decisions regarding the fate of the Saint John's bread program.

New Beginnings

Under Father Gordon's direction, Jerry Mead initiated three efforts to revive the program. The first of these was to find a new partner with whom to pursue Father Walter's dream of a frozen bread that could be baked at home. Red Owl had dropped the frozen product in 1970, so contacts were made with Royal Pantry Foods, "a new company looking for new ideas."[13] When Mead met with Royal Pantry officials in late 1973, they argued that to launch a new frozen bread product required "a sizeable advertising budget." Since neither party was so inclined, Royal Pantry offered a low-cost alternative. They would develop the product, test it with some of their major buyers, and then, if the results were positive, see if sales could be developed without advertising.[14] Father Gordon was ecstatic, responding that "this is the best news we have had yet."[15]

The new team's second tactic in the struggle to restore Father Walter's empire was to add new firms, known as "blenders," as sources for the bread mix. While Pillsbury remained a major supplier, the abbey made agreements with the Philip Orth Company of Wisconsin, Richardson and Holland of Washington, and Brechet and Richter of Minnesota to carry out the same manufacturing/distribution functions in their areas. This change reduced some shipping costs but was motivated primarily by the sense that Pillsbury salesmen weren't aggressively promoting a product that constituted only a small fraction of their sales. As Mead explained, he hoped that with the smaller blenders, the opportunity to sell 10,000 to 20,000 bags a year would "really mean something."[16] The blenders also offered the abbey a welcome chance to increase its royalty: the new suppliers paid Saint John's $3.00 per 100 pound bag sold, or double the amount received from Russell-Miller/Peavey and Pillsbury.[17]

Finally, Saint John's launched a renewed effort to place the famous loaf on the shelves of grocery store chains, using a much more aggressive and expensive strategy than Father Walter had employed. Jerry Mead, freed from some of his on-campus responsibilities as Food Service Director by the hiring of a new assistant, devoted about half of his time in 1974 to promoting Johnnie Bread.[18] Working with the blenders, he established substantial contacts with at least nine grocery chains in states from Iowa to Massachusetts.[19] If a client showed interest, Mead acted as the intermediary between the mix supplier and the store, coordinated advertising, offered to teach the staff about Saint John's bread, and made sure that each store manager and bakery manager received "a set of [four] decorator Saint John's Bread cocktail glasses" for arranging the desired displays.[20] In addition to such gifts, Saint John's provided all of the promotional materials for in-store displays, including buttons for employees to wear during the campaign, and paid for the initial newspaper and television ads. Since the cost of the latter in one case was estimated at $2,500, it was clear that re-starting the bread program would require a much greater investment than Father Walter's original efforts.[21] Still, given that one of the chains Mead contacted had ninety stores, the opportunity seemed worth the risk. As Father Gordon noted in June 1974, "our bread operation seems to be making good and steady forward progress—we're very optimistic."[22]

As they sought new clients in grocery chains and elsewhere, Jerry Mead and Father Gordon adapted to the commercial culture by giving away a variety of mementoes emblazoned with the old Pillsbury-designed Franciscan monk. Decision makers got cocktail glasses, cigarette lighters, and pocket knives, while buttons and decals were distributed more freely. Bakers were appropriately wooed with Saint John's inscribed bowl scrapers to be used while mixing the dough. (Courtesy of Saint John's Abbey Archives)

A Benedictine Partnership

While the neophytes were trying to resurrect what was left of Father Walter's empire, a heavenly gift fell into their laps courtesy of the Benedictines of the Holy Cross Abbey of Cañon City, Colorado. In October 1972, Brother Michael Murray, the Holy Cross procurator, dropped in unexpectedly to talk to Father Gordon. It seemed that Father Gordon had mentioned something about what Saint John's was doing at a meeting of Benedictine procurators, and had piqued Brother Michael's interest in bread franchising.[23] It was this conversation that would ultimately lead to an arrangement whereby Holy Cross would franchise a product called "Abbey Bread," using the Saint John's mix and splitting the royalties.

At first, the negotiations between the two abbeys proceeded smoothly. By early 1973, the deal was sufficiently advanced for Father Gordon to give his blessing to Brother Michael's solicitation of bakeries in Colorado.[24] Soon, however, contract details began to threaten the Benedictine harmony. The Holy Cross Chapter very much wanted the right to market a frozen Abbey Bread, but Father Gordon, evidently sharing Father Walter's vision of the frozen potential, successfully insisted on exclusive rights for Saint John's.[25] An even more bitterly contested issue was the length of the contract. Saint John's proposed a two-year deal, but Brother Michael argued that if Holy Cross was going to put a lot of effort into developing franchises, a five-year agreement was more reasonable. Although Saint John's lawyer Kevin Hughes (SJU '58) strongly defended the shorter period, Father Gordon gave in, encouraged no doubt by a veiled threat from Brother Michael revealing that he had been talking to Pillsbury about developing a Holy Cross recipe "that we could market with less difficulty than we have experienced thus far."[26] Finally, in June 1973, a contract was signed, giving Holy Cross Abbey the right to franchise Abbey Bread with the "The Loaf That Became a Legend" slogan in retail bakeries in Colorado, Wyoming, New Mexico, and Texas. Pillsbury would supply the mix, collecting a $3.00 per 100 pound bag royalty that would be split, with $2.50 going to Holy Cross and $0.50 to Saint John's.[27]

With the contract in place, Holy Cross started wooing customers and soon made a major conquest. Safeway, one of the largest chains in the area, agreed to carry Abbey Bread in its Rocky Mountain outlets and to add stores on the West

Coast if the reception was favorable.[28] Both Benedictine houses were ecstatic over the connection with Safeway, for as Father Gordon noted, "Safeway is largest $ chain in US," and access to all of its stores might mean "looking at 6,000,000 loaf/year."[29] The Holy Cross contract was quickly amended in early 1974 to give the Colorado abbey the rights to Safeway stores nationwide.[30]

Within a year, it appeared that Safeway would fulfill all the dreams of the two abbeys. In April 1975, Brother Michael signed an agreement that promised to add 985 Safeway stores to the 621 in the chain that already sold Abbey Bread. Like Father Walter before him, Brother Michael saw this as just the beginning. He expected the remaining 367 Safeway stores in the United States to join as well, and was contemplating adding the chain's outlets in Canada, Australia, England, and Germany. With the expanded prospects, Brother Michael expected to sell over 3,000,000 sacks of mix in the coming year.[31]

If Brother Michael's predictions had been correct, Saint John's would have earned approximately $1,500,000 per year from its share. Unfortunately, that was not the case. The promised expansion into new Safeways was repeatedly delayed, and in many cases never accomplished. Ultimately, Abbey Bread's trajectory mirrored that of the original loaf, though on a smaller scale. In fiscal year 1976, the Minnesota abbey's royalties from the Holy Cross sales were $6,838. After three years of steady decline, the 1979 totals were $1,173, or barely a drop in the bucket.[32]

A Sputtering Start

In the four years after Father Walter's death, the Tavis-Mead team had worked very hard to resurrect bread sales, taking a new run at frozen bread and chain stores, while bringing in new blenders to supplement Pillsbury and signing the agreement with Holy Cross Abbey. By 1975, the Holy Cross connection appeared to have great potential, but results elsewhere were more mixed.

On the positive side, bread sales had increased substantially, with gross income rising from about $11,000 in Father Walter's last year to just under $34,000 in fiscal year 1975.[33] Some of the increase was due to the Holy Cross royalties, but the primary factor was sales by the new blenders. They accounted for about $20,000 of the 1975 revenues, while Pillsbury's traditional clients contributed somewhat less than the $11,000 they had in 1971.[34] Clearly the decision to recruit new allies had been helpful.

The new team's other initiatives, however, had not turned out so well. The frozen bread program with Royal Pantry led only to repeated frustration. Father Gordon expected a product on the market by early 1974, but, by 1976, only the promotional materials were ready.[35] Frustrated, in August Father Gordon wrote to a Duluth acquaintance to ask her advice on how to approach frozen-pizza pioneer Jeno Palucci for help. Father Gordon's notes on a follow-up telephone conversation read: "Write to him direct. Give explanation of what in mind. Bring an Italian Priest with us. Better have [Father Raymond] Pedrizetti write."[36] Despite this effort, there is no evidence that the frozen bread effort was ever revived.

Jerry Mead's frenetic pursuit of new opportunities in various grocery chains was almost as disappointing. Out of nine firms that received major solicitations in 1974, at most only four ever baked a loaf of Johnnie Bread.[37] The others received involved proposals and watched product demonstrations, but still said, "No thank you." The major participants later offered differing views on why the effort didn't take off. Mead insisted that the central problem was that Saint John's was unwilling to make the substantial investment in advertising required by the stores.[38] Father Gordon's interpretation, however, was that Johnnie Bread had lost its uniqueness as the market had changed: "To come in with a two-grain bread

Although commercial sales failed to take off as hoped in the mid-1970s, demand remained steady at home. The caption in this 1975 yearbook photograph asked, "Fresh Johnnie Bread, what more could a man ask?" (Photo courtesy of Saint John's University Archives)

when there were seven-grain breads on the market was hardly anything new."[39] Regardless of which factor was most significant, it is clear that without either advertising funds or a unique niche, the famous loaf had even less ability to swim against market trends in the 1970s than it had had a decade before with Father Walter. Given that the new efforts brought only small gains despite significant promotional expenses (including half of Mead's salary), Father Gordon realized that "we just had to change our approach in order to survive."[40] By November 1975, Saint John's had "dropped our sales campaign to sell to grocery chains and wholesale bakeries."[41]

Shifting Gears

Rather than bucking the barriers involved in trying to sell the famous loaf to individual consumers, Father Gordon decided to pursue direct sales of the mix to institutions such as schools and hospitals. The roots of this reorientation stretched back to Mead's 1974 efforts to find new clients. During his travels, he had spent some time in Alabama, where he had worked prior to coming to Saint John's. While there, he happened to run into Austin Hansen, an old friend whose Atlanta-based firm supplied equipment and some food products to institutional clients across the South.[42] Anxious to help out, Hansen provided Mead access to some of his accounts, and the team gained modest success. In late 1974 and early 1975, Mead sold about 18,000 pounds of the bread mix to the public schools in Raleigh, North Carolina, and Birmingham, Alabama.[43] Seeing an opportunity that no longer seemed available in retail sales, the decision makers at Saint John's decided sometime in the summer of 1975 to make a major effort to use Hansen's contacts to pursue institutional sales.[44] To do so, Mead's role was redefined. Instead of splitting his time between campus responsibilities and helping blenders open supermarket doors, Mead became a full-time off-campus salesman, traveling with Hansen to crack the institutional market in the Southeast.[45]

The plan was to offer institutions the mix, which could be used not only for the standard white and dark breads, but also as a base for dinner rolls, biscuits, hot dog buns, and even sweet rolls.[46] By baking a variety of goods on site, clients could avoid the higher cost of commercial bakery products. More importantly, the mix eliminated the need for baking expertise in kitchens that rarely had professionally trained staff.[47] With a mix, instructions could be broken down to the most basic level: "what we did was we said we'll take a num-

111

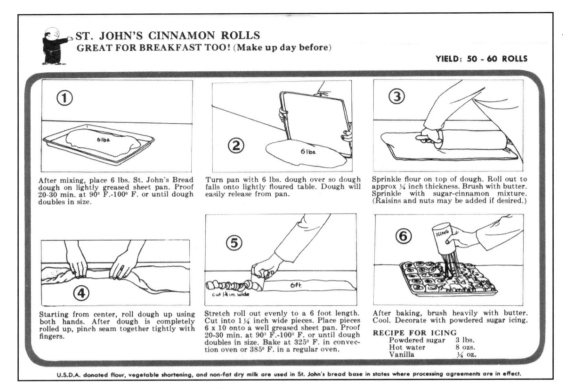

ST. JOHN'S CINNAMON ROLLS
GREAT FOR BREAKFAST TOO! (Make up day before)

YIELD: 50 - 60 ROLLS

① After mixing, place 6 lbs. St. John's Bread dough on lightly greased sheet pan. Proof 20-30 min. at 90° F.-100° F. or until dough doubles in size.

② Turn pan with 6 lbs. dough over so dough falls onto lightly floured table. Dough will easily release from pan.

③ Sprinkle flour on top of dough. Roll out to approx ¼ inch thickness. Brush with butter. Sprinkle with sugar-cinnamon mixture. (Raisins and nuts may be added if desired.)

④ Starting from center, roll dough up using both hands. After dough is completely rolled up, pinch seam together tightly with fingers.

⑤ Stretch roll out evenly to a 6 foot length. Cut into 1¼ inch wide pieces. Place pieces 6 x 10 onto a well greased sheet pan. Proof 20-30 min. at 90° F.-100° F. or until dough doubles in size. Bake at 325° F. in convection oven or 385° F. in a regular oven.

⑥ After baking, brush heavily with butter. Cool. Decorate with powdered sugar icing.

RECIPE FOR ICING
Powdered sugar	3 lbs.
Hot water	8 ozs.
Vanilla	¼ oz.

U.S.D.A. donated flour, vegetable shortening, and non-fat dry milk are used in St. John's bread base in states where processing agreements are in effect.

Risk-proof production was a key factor for institutional customers. The base mix for Saint John's white and dark bread came in color-coded sacks with full instructions on the amount of base, flour, yeast, and water to mix depending on the amount of end product desired. Since versatility was also highly desirable, Jerry Mead gave demonstrations in institutional kitchens across the nation, convincing them that they could use the base mix for products other than bread. As a reminder, Mead provided detailed recipe cards such as the one pictured for cinnamon rolls made from the white mix. (Courtesy of Jerry Mead)

ber ten can of Saint John's bread mix and a number ten can of flour and a number ten can of water."[48] Once Mead learned to color code the bags so that employees didn't combine the white and dark mixes, the system was "simplified as easy as it could be."[49] Bags of Johnnie Bread mix thus provided a great solution to the needs of institutional clients in a field where there appeared to be less competition than in retail sales. Furthermore, unbeknownst to Father Gordon, Mead's personal characteristics made him a particularly good salesman among the largely female institutional kitchen staffs. As a woman who witnessed Mead's techniques at a Minnesota school demonstration remembered, "The cooks loved him because he was drop-dead handsome and laid on the Southern charm."[50]

Father Gordon's willingness to initiate this new effort was enhanced by the presence of Austin Hansen. By a strange quirk, Hansen had developed an affection for Saint John's long before he began to promote Johnnie Bread. While growing up in Elgin, Illinois, Hansen admired the local high school basketball star, Jim Smith. Hansen followed Smith's career as a college player, and when Jim began his long tenure at Saint

John's as head basketball coach, Hansen studied the school. As a result, Father Gordon believed that Hansen "really wanted to help Saint John's."[51] More important, Hansen also brought significant business benefits to the endeavor. He had an established firm, with a knowledgeable work force and strong connections throughout the Southeast. Since Hansen "was already known to the customer," Father Gordon explained, "it looked like it had more possibility than the hit and miss course we had been on."[52] Despite the increased overhead, the new venture seemed like a great opportunity.

While the pursuit of institutional sales in the Southeast made great business sense, the new direction meant a significant departure from Father Walter's vision in several ways. On the most basic level, Jerry Mead's assignment meant that for the first time the program had a full-time employee, and moreover one who was not even based in Collegeville. This meant ignoring both Father Walter's vision of the tax code, and his penchant for avoiding significant overhead. Furthermore, Father Walter's early campaigns had focused on those who were most likely to have some prior knowledge or empathy for the source of the bread. In contrast, pursuing clients in the Southeast meant moving into totally alien territory; one wonders what Southern Baptist cooks made of the cartoon Franciscans that Mead used in his demonstrations on the virtues of the mix. Along the same lines, Father Walter had always promoted Johnnie Bread as an integral part of an historic Benedictine tradition. Institutional sales meant that the ultimate consumer of the bread would have no sense of that message, while the buyers of the mix were certainly more moved by pragmatic issues such as cost, versatility, and ease of use. More important, one of Father Walter's core goals in making Johnnie Bread commercially available was to maintain contact with alumni, which was clearly out of the question with institutional sales. Finally, it was very clear that Father Walter also wanted to sell the famous loaf in order to help Americans learn to appreciate "real" bread. The new program largely abandoned this missionary goal, since the multiple uses of the mix meant that relatively few loaves of the classic dark Johnnie Bread would be produced. Ultimately, the emphasis on institutional accounts in the mid-1970s reflected a much more narrowly commercial spirit, shorn of Father Walter's other objectives. While the original program had always had fund-raising as a critical component, the revived program was centered on that goal.

113

Institutional Sales Begin

Through late 1975 and early 1976, a number of steps were taken to pursue the opportunity presented by institutional sales in the Southeast. After making Hansen the exclusive broker for Saint John's Bread in the area, Mead and Father Gordon chose Griffith Food Service as the local blender of the mix.[53] Using the Atlanta-based Griffith saved freight costs, but also brought in the drive and enthusiasm of Griffith's National Sales Director John Rymer. Throughout the winter of 1975-1976, Rymer got Griffith plants ready to manufacture the Saint John's mix, and drilled his sales force in how they could augment Hansen's efforts. At the same time, Rymer, Hansen, and Mead did baking demonstrations for countless schools, hospitals, and prisons across the South.[54] Finally, Hansen and Mead worked to get the mix accepted as part of the United States Department of Agriculture Commodity Blending program.[55] This was a key step, for with this approval, the schools could provide Griffith with government subsidized shortening and milk to be included in the mix. The schools, therefore, not only got the mix at a lower price, but were able to turn unwieldy surplus commodities into an easy-to-prepare product with multiple uses.[56]

While Hansen, Rymer, and Mead devoted a lot of energy to finding clients for the mix, their efforts reaped few immediate results. Even the ever optimistic Rymer admitted in March 1976 that "there has not been a large amount of new business." Nevertheless, he insisted that "we have made tremendous progress" in establishing contacts.[57] That effort, he was sure, would pay off soon. By May, Rymer was predicting sales for fiscal year 1977 that would net Saint John's $142,350 in royalties.[58]

For those in Collegeville, this enthusiasm must have been as welcome as a seventy-degree day in March, but as any Minnesotan knows, early spring warmth is not to be trusted. While Rymer waxed optimistic, Father Gordon saw a blizzard approaching. The central problem was the overhead associated with the new program. By late spring, Father Gordon was so worried by mounting costs that he moved from urging Mead to find ways to trim costs to proposing that Mead cease being a salaried employee of Saint John's and instead accept the role as Johnnie Bread's exclusive broker in Alabama. Mead found the suggestion "unfair" and re-iterated his belief that the profits would soon roll in.[59] Father Gordon relented temporarily but knew that changes would be necessary.

The depths of the problem were amply apparent when the books were closed on fiscal year 1976 at the end of June. Gross income was up thirty-eight percent over the previous year to $54,827, but expenses jumped sixty-two percent to $89,420, leaving the program with a net loss of $34,593 for the year.[60] Since the contributions from Pillsbury's traditional clients, Holy Cross, and the various blenders remained pretty stable, the key to the altered picture lay with the institutional sales program. The royalties from Griffith Foods hit $16,600 in the first year of the Mead-Hansen-Rymer effort, which was a nice addition, but unfortunately it fell far below the $75,000 Father Gordon had projected in the budget. Furthermore, while the Griffith income had fallen short, start-up costs charged to the program had exceeded expectations slightly.

Much of the increased cost in 1976 was due to the expanded effort to recruit institutional buyers across the Southeast. With Mead as a full-time salesman, both salary and travel costs jumped. Also, there were substantial commissions to be paid to Hansen and other brokers, as well as thousands of dollars required to mount presentations at conventions. At the same time, however, the sudden surge in costs in fiscal year 1976 was also more apparent than real, for it also reflected new accounting techniques. During the late 1960s and early 1970s few costs were charged to the program.[61] The lack of precise accounting was appropriate in the years when many individual monks like Father Walter worked at multiple tasks for income that all went into a common pot. Spurred both by increased complexity of the enterprise and the need to account for the "real" money paid a growing corps of lay people, both the abbey and university began to upgrade their financial procedures in the early 1970s. For the bread program, the change occurred in fiscal year 1975, when the enterprise received more $60,000 from the university's Debt Service Reserve in order to pay off old debts that had accumulated since Father Walter's death.[62] Then, in the next year, significant new overhead charges were made against bread profits. For example, during the preceding year, Mead's extensive travel had cost the program only sixty dollars, office expenses were listed at $264, and there were no charges for staff or telephone. With the new accounting in fiscal year 1976, travel rocketed to $29,014, and the other three items totaled $9,744.08.[63] Selling bread had not only become more expensive, but the full costs of doing business were now obvious to everyone, especially to Father Gordon and cost-conscious critics in the Business Office.

115

While Father Gordon reflected on the hemorrhage revealed in the budget data for fiscal year 1976, he was under pressure to invest even more. John Rymer continued to insist that "Saint John's is going to be #1 in Food Service," but only if the opportunity were exploited aggressively.[64] To this end, Rymer wanted Saint John's to expand the Southeastern focus to a national program, and to invest in the development of an additional line of mixes for pie crust, waffles, and cakes.

Rymer's optimism was tempting but raised two significant issues in addition to the obvious problem of investing more money in an endeavor whose success was less than certain. The first of these was the old question of identity: was it appropriate or desirable for Saint John's as a religious/educational institution to be nationally known for a commercial product? While it isn't clear how widespread the concern was, it clearly came up, for Father Gordon's handwritten notes during a discussion read: "gut questions - is it what SJU wants. To be known as developer of most widely selling bread."[65] Although commercial notoriety might be unseemly, there was the marvelous allure of financial security insured by a successful product. In his notes, Father Gordon mused "Xian [Christian] Bros Brandy is the kind of thing we could be," and apparently settled the issue for himself with the conclusion, "Xian Bros live with it."[66] If the Christian Brothers could marry a religious vocation and commercial success, why not the Benedictines?

Rymer's call for an even larger Saint John's commitment in pursuit of a national program also made the question of the abbey's tax exempt status more salient again. When Father Gordon and Saint John's lawyer Kevin Hughes had discussed this issue in 1975, prior to the decision to pursue institutional sales, they had concluded that they should "not be terribly worried because [we] have one employee."[67] If they kept the Saint John's part "small, small" and got the manufacturers and/or brokers to do most of the work, they believed that they could avoid running afoul of the Internal Revenue Service.[68] Even so, they were sufficiently worried so that the agreements with Hansen and Rymer were made verbally "so as to stay out of direct business involvement as much as possible."[69] Clearly, mounting a national campaign would force Saint John's to face the tax issue squarely. Father Gordon later recalled that he was prepared to handle this by creating a separate taxable entity for the bread program, but evidence from the 1970s indicates less assurance.[70] Even if a separate corporation had resolved the tax problem, tying Saint John's to a full-fledged for-profit enterprise undoubtedly would have exacerbated the issue of identity for many.

While the tax and identity issues were significant, Father Gordon ultimately decided against a Saint John's-led national program because he was unwilling to risk more money. As he told the Regents Finance Committee, "We all feel that Saint John's has put as much as it can afford into start-up costs."[71] Given this reality, yet still hoping for success in the bread venture, Father Gordon looked for alternatives.

Cutting Back

Rather than increasing the Saint John's role in the summer of 1976, Father Gordon decided to let Hansen and Rymer assume full responsibility for taking the program nationwide. This would mean a smaller share of any royalties for Saint John's, but, by turning the enterprise over to the Georgia team and withdrawing Jerry Mead, Father Gordon could minimize both the economic drain and the possibility of violating IRS guidelines.[72] Father Gordon had contemplated this approach a year earlier but at that time had decided that a significant Saint John's role was necessary because Hansen lacked the staff to succeed outside of his Southeastern base.[73] A year's expenditures had changed his vision; Father Gordon was now willing to accept whatever results Hansen and Rymer could produce so long as the drain on the Collegeville treasury was curtailed.

After receiving permission from the executive committee of the Board of Regents, Father Gordon worked out the new arrangements with Dogwood Marketing Group, as Hansen and Rymer named their enterprise. Under the terms of the formal contract signed in December 1976, Dogwood became the sole national marketing agent for the famous loaf and related mixes save in a few areas where Saint John's had pre-existing contracts.[74] As sole agents, Dogwood was responsible for developing and servicing new markets, as well as working with Pillsbury and the other blenders producing the mix, assuring quality, and handling all legal aspects.[75] Clients would be charged royalties ranging from $1.00 on non-bread mixes up to $2.75 for the standard white and dark loaf; of these, Saint John's would receive between fifty cents and $1.50 per fifty-pound sack sold.[76] Collegeville's contribution to marketing was greatly decreased, with the order promising to pay $3,000 per year toward booths at conventions and to provide "a program coordinator" two or three times a month "to fill the public relations function."[77] As Father Gordon explained, the new arrangement "doesn't mean we are disinterested or uninvolved, but we are not going to be actively involved in selling."[78] Actually, while the direct contribution to convention costs flowed from the assumptions of the mid-1970s program, having the Saint John's role limited to a periodic public relations appearance was very much in keeping with the spirit of Father Walter's regime.

Despite the dramatic reduction of the Saint John's commitment, both parties seemed to be quite optimistic about the future. Father Gordon saw the new arrangements as turning "a corner into a totally new era of Saint John's Bread operation" and predicted net revenues in the transitional fiscal year of 1977 of at least $25,000.[79] Hansen and Rymer at Dogwood were even more optimistic, agreeing to give Saint John's the right to terminate the agreement unless sales increased five percent per year from an initial base of $60,000 in royalties.[80] Since Hansen's efforts in 1976 had delivered only $16,660 to Collegeville, the Dogwood partners clearly had sold themselves on the product's potential.

With Hansen and Rymer pushing hard, Dogwood was able to sell Johnnie Bread mixes to a number of new institutional clients in 1977. School districts in North Carolina, Missouri, and Arizona signed on, as well as several Southern universities, some prisons, and a ship supply company.[81] The result was doubling of royalties from the Dogwood sector, to a total of $32,627 in fiscal year 1977.[82]

Unfortunately, the bottom line for 1977 was scarcely better than its predecessor, with Saint John's still absorbing a loss of $20,840.[83] Since the new arrangements with Dogwood came into effect only half way through the fiscal year, expenses remained high, dropping from $89,420 in 1976 to $71,006 in 1977. To make matters worse, overall income actually fell $4,000 to $50,166 as declining Holy Cross contributions and the evaporation of grocery chain sales more than offset the gains from Dogwood.

The End of the Commercial Trail

Although the continued red ink was of great concern to Father Gordon, he must have been optimistic about Johnnie Bread's prospects for the upcoming fiscal year. After all, Dogwood was making inroads, plus Saint John's had curtailed its expenses by re-assigning Jerry Mead and largely withdrawing from the sales effort. The good news for fiscal year 1978 was that the famous loaf turned a profit for Saint John's; the bad news was that it was only $6,049, and the disastrous news was that sales had collapsed. Gross income was only $19,099, or a thirty-eight-percent drop from the previous year.[84] The situation was so bad that, in the spring of 1978, Griffith Food Service, which had played a central role in the Dogwood effort as the Southeastern supplier of the mix, bailed out, acknowledging that Johnnie Bread was a "good product" with "a great name behind it," but "the situation didn't materialize properly."[85]

Griffith's departure further disrupted a shaky program, but Austin Hansen and Father Gordon kept the faith a little longer. In the fall of 1978, Father Gordon reported that "Austin and his daughter Terri have been recapturing some of our losses. We are still a long way from those first initial penetrations of the market that we accomplished with Griffith. But, it does seem to be coming back. In fact, Austin is so enthusiastic that he thinks he has to keep reminding me that he is not being carried away like Jerry Mead and John Rymer had been. He really expects the thing to pop and soon. When that occurs we will all begin to breathe more easily."[86]

Again, the optimism proved unfounded. From Jerry Mead's perspective, Hansen remained hampered by the absence of Saint John's financial support, plus Austin lacked the baking expertise that Jerry had used to convince clients of the mix's versatility.[87] Others, however, blamed the failure on external forces. Pillsbury, General Mills, and other large firms quickly realized that Saint John's institutional program met a real need, and, therefore, had significant potential.[88] As a result, they developed their own line of multiple-use mixes and used their superior resources to overwhelm small players like Dogwood. As Father Gordon recalled, "We were out of business before we knew what had happened."[89]

It may very well be that Saint John's was doomed in such a battle regardless, but the 1970s strategy made it particularly vulnerable. Whereas the 1950s program had emphasized the distinctiveness of the famous loaf, in the 1970s clients were offered convenience and cost effectiveness in products that, for the most part, could not make any claim to unique flavor or texture. Sweet rolls made with Saint John's mix were like any other sweet roll. Similarly, where the earlier program had worked the mystique of an Old World tradition, those buying the 1970s product were offered only a cartoon monk as part of a sales pitch focused on other factors and delivered by a Southern-raised layman. They thus could hardly be expected to make choices based on status or sentiment as had been the case in Father Walter's day. In short, since the 1970s product was promoted solely for its commercial value to consumers who had little reason to add other factors to the accounting, it was especially vulnerable to the kind of price and service advantages possessed by the big suppliers in the market.

By the end of 1979, Father Gordon's efforts to use Johnnie Bread as a source of significant revenue were over. Despite Austin Hansen's best efforts, royalties from that side of the enterprise were only $3,191 in fiscal year 1979, or one tenth of what they had been only two years earlier.[90] Closer to home, with sales from the flagship Zinsmaster bakeries slumping and the Holy Cross contributions essentially ended, Pillsbury's royalty payments fell to less than half of what they had been three years earlier.[91] Total royalties were barely over $11,000, and the program was once again charged with a loss, this time of $8,705.

When Father Gordon and his team began their struggle to revive Johnnie Bread's commercial potential in the early 1970s, it seemed a very logical thing to do. After all, they had a quality product that a few years earlier had been quite successful. Furthermore, without a thorough analysis of the barriers facing a specialty loaf, it must have been relatively easy to assume that the sales decline could be traced to the belief that "Father Walter was not a businessman," and to the obvious reality of his declining health.[92] It seemed reasonable that an aggressive strategy and new energy would yield positive results. When their early sallies revealed intense competition from similar products, as well as the same problems of in-store bakeries and increasing scale that faced Father Walter, Father Gordon quickly recognized the handwriting on the wall. Seeking opportunity in an apparently open area, Father Gordon and Jerry Mead dropped Father Walter's dream of providing a unique product in the retail arena for the promise of serving institutional clients with a full range of products. The strategy seemed entirely appropriate, but once again it turned out that Johnnie Bread simply lacked the resources to compete against larger players. In the end, the attempt to revive the Johnnie Bread enterprise had cost its sponsors sleepless nights, dashed hopes, and at least $58,089 over the five years from 1974 through 1979.[93]

Back to Collegeville

As the famous loaf headed into the 1980s, it was available to the larger public only at a handful of Minnesota grocery stores. These firms baked the bread themselves, using the mix supplied by Brechet and Richter of Golden Valley, who had become one of the blenders in the early 1970s. Loyal alums sustained enough demand to keep the product available, but sales weren't exactly booming. The Johnnie Bread revenue stream was so thin that neither party noticed when the new management team that took over Brechet and Richter in 1984 forgot to continue royalty payments. When the mistake was finally discovered a decade later, the total royalties owed amounted to only $19,700, or slightly less than

While the taste and texture of the campus-baked Johnnie Bread remained as earlier alumni remembered it, other things on campus had changed by 1996, when this photo was taken. Sexton Commons (center) and the Art Building (far right), as well as new dorms such as Virgil Michel (below Sexton) and others in Flynntown (outside photo) had been added. Those returning for reunions would encounter a more stunning transformation: women were no longer rare behind the pine curtain. By the 1990s, cooperation between Saint John's and the College of Saint Benedict had evolved into a unique relationship. Each school retained its distinctiveness, while students shared curriculum, faculty, classrooms, and other facilities in a thoroughly integrated academic experience. Saint John's is even approaching gender equity in the number of public restrooms. (Photo courtesy of Saint John's Public Information Office)

Two traditions among the changes: Johnnie Football and Johnnie Bread. While hundreds of loaves are sold each weekend in the fall, alumni and other visitors usually carry more than 1,500 loaves away as they leave after Homecoming. (Photo courtesy of Saint John's University Archives)

Rich Ruprecht, the latest in a long line of bakers stretching back to Brother William Baldus, carries half a batch of new dough from the mixer to the table where he will form it into approximately thirty loaves. Working from late afternoon deep into the night, on a normal shift, Rich produces more than 120 loaves of the traditional Johnnie Bread, plus rolls and other breads, all to be consumed the next day. (Photo by Ken Jones)

$2,000 per year. While both Father Gordon and Brechet and Richter President Tom Moore stopped short of offering hopes for a resurgence, Moore did note that sales were growing at about seven percent per year in the early 1990s.[94]

While Johnnie Bread is no longer widely available, the traditional loaf continues to be produced on campus. Each evening, Rich Ruprecht, who has been the chief baker since 1989, begins his shift by combining a fifty-pound bag of mix with a fifty-pound sack of white flour, yeast, and water. When the dough has reached the approved consistency (tested by Rich's experienced touch), he removes it from the mixer, and forms sixty-three to sixty-five loaves by hand.[95] Once it has risen, the classic loaf is cooked on revolving trays in a twelve-foot-long oven that was used by the early German nuns. It is this baking process, plus Rich's slow mixing, that produces the characteristic dense loaf with a tough crust that visitors to campus remember.[96]

The traditional loaf is, of course, served with every meal just as it was when it was baked by monks or by French, Ger-

122

man, and Mexican nuns. Like their fathers and grandfathers, however, modern students know that Johnnie Bread hits the spot outside the refectory as well. Whether it is an individual cram session, or floor meeting in the dorm, slabs of the traditional loaf smeared with peanut butter and jam are always in high demand.[97] Even monks are not immune; the president has been observed grabbing a loaf as he passes through the bakery on his way back to his room after a long day. Late at night, as the smell of fresh-baked bread wafts across campus, the temptation grows for anyone still up; with an unlocked back door, Rich's visitors include everyone from bored security guards to cramming students.[98]

To meet the on-campus demand, the kitchens produce the equivalent of 200 loaves per day during the school year, most of it in the form of the traditional dark loaf.[99] As Father Walter knew, however, the bread holds a particularly important place in the hearts of many alumni. Each year before Homecoming Weekend, Rich Ruprecht puts in a couple of fourteen hour days to produce 2,500 loaves, over 1,500 of which are purchased and carried home to extend the nostalgia. Even when large numbers of alumni aren't around, visitors snap up fifty to sixty two-pound loaves of the traditional dark bread every day.[100] Most buy a loaf or two, but some cart off a dozen or more for friends or for the freezer. In addition, since late 1996,

The Benedictine nuns who settled in Saint Joseph in 1863 and later founded the College of Saint Benedict also developed their own unique bread. Although far less publicized than its Collegeville counterpart, Bennie Bread has delighted students and visitors for decades. Embodying the coordinate relationship between the two schools that had evolved by 1987 when this photo was taken, presidents Sister Colman O'Connell (left) of the College of Saint Benedict and Saint John's Father Hilary Thimmesh (right) jointly presented their campus' distinctive loaves to Minneapolis Mayor Don Frazer (center). (Photo courtesy of Saint John's University Archives)

123

those with bread machines can recreate the famous loaf using a mix promoted by Dining Service Director, Dave Schoenberg. It is a far cry from Father Walter's dream, but those outside of Collegeville do still have some access to the famous loaf.

Ultimately, as it was with Brother Wolfgang almost 140 years ago, Johnnie Bread remains an essential part of Benedictine sharing on many levels. Whether it is the loaf that a Benedictine visitor invariably brings as a gift, thick slices as part of the meal in the campus dining room, or Johnnie Bread as communion wafers in the abbey church, the taste and texture of the famous loaf beckons people to share in the humanity and inclusiveness of the Benedictine community.

Knowing that part of Johnnie Bread's mystique lay in its "fresh from the oven" taste, Father Walter repeatedly sought a frozen-dough version that could be baked at home. Though he failed in his quest, his dream was realized in late 1996 when Saint John's Dining Service Director Dave Schoenberg (above) made the traditional dark loaf available in a mix for home bread machines. By the summer of 1997, visitors to Saint John's were buying as many loaves in this new format as they were purchasing in the standard ready-to-eat form. (Photo by Ken Jones)

Notes

1. Interview with Tom LeNeau, July 22, 1996.
2. Interview with Tom LeNeau.
3. LeNeau to Moran, May 27, 1971, Abbey Archives, 318, Bread File.
4. LeNeau to Petersen, March 30, 1971, Abbey Archives, 318, Bread File.
5. Mead to McCall, October 13, 1972, Abbey Archives, 315, Bread.
6. Interview with Tom LeNeau, July 22, 1996; Interview with Lee Hanley, July 11, 1996.
7. Interview with Lee Hanley, July 11, 1996.
8. Mead to McCall, October 13, 1972, Abbey Archives, 315, Bread.
9. Interview with Father Gordon Tavis, August 9, 1994.
10. Tavis to Hall, July 24, 1972, Abbey Archives, 315, Bread.
11. Tavis to Anderson, August 17, 1972, Abbey Archives, 315, Bread.
12. Interview with Father Gervase Soukup, July 7, 1995.
13. "Meeting with Jerry Hanna and Jim Hall," January 8 (no year), Abbey Archives, 318, Bread Files.
14. Anderson to Tavis, December 19, 1973, 318, Saint John's Bread.
15. Tavis to Murray, December 17, 1973, Abbey Archives, Holy Cross Abbey Contract.

16. Interview with Jerry Mead, September 12, 1996.

17. The Pillsbury agreement was $3.00 per 100 pound bag, but $1.50 of this went into a fund that the baker could then draw on for advertising. (See Eckhardt to Abbey, June 3, 1975, Abbey Archives, 318, Dogwood Contract.) There is nothing in the Orth contract about an advertising fund, so it appears that the Abbey received the entire $3.00 per bag. Agreement with Orth, April 3, 1974, Abbey Archives, 318, Bread Strategy.

18. Todd Mueller, "Saint John's Sells Bread to Make Dough," *Record*, February 28, 1975, p. 5. It isn't clear how much time Mead actually devoted to Johnnie Bread, but about half of his salary was charged to the bread program. Budget Printout, June 30, 1976, Abbey Archives, 318, Bread Budgets.

19. Interview with Jerry Mead, September 12, 1996; see, for example, contract with Hinky-Dinky Stores, August 21, 1974, Abbey Archives, 317, Hinky-Dinky.

20. Mead to Lavengood, July18 1974, Abbey Archives, 317, Eisner's Food Stores.

21. Mead to Lavengood, July 18 1974,.

22. Tavis to Murray, June 14, 1974, Abbey Archives, 318, Holy Cross Contract.

23. Murray to Tavis, October 20, 1972, Abbey Archives, 318, Holy Cross Contract; Interview with Father Gordon Tavis, August 9, 1994.

24. Tavis to "To Whom It May Concern," February 19, 1973, Abbey Archives, 318, Holy Cross Contract.

25. Murray to Tavis, February 23, 1973, Abbey Archives, 318, Holy Cross Contract; License Agreement, 1973 and 1975 versions, Abbey Archives, 318, Holy Cross Contract.

26. Murray to Tavis, June 19, 1973,.

27. License Agreement, 1973, Abbey Archives, 318, Holy Cross Contract.

28. Murray to Tavis, March 5, 1974.

29. Handwritten notes on conversation with Brother Michael and Jerry Hanna of Pillsbury, May 6, 1974, Abbey Archives, 318, Holy Cross Contract.

30. License Agreement, March 5, 1974, 318, Holy Cross Contract.

31. This success raised the same income tax concerns for Brother Michael as Father Walter had faced earlier. He informed Father Gordon that "the lawyers felt that it is not a matter that should be put on any stationery or written at any one time." Murray to Tavis, April 8, 1975, Abbey Archives, 318, Holy Cross Contract.

32. Account Sheets, Abbey Archives, 320, Pillsbury Sales Data.

33. Total expenses in fiscal year 1975 were $33,935, so the official

net profit was one dollar. $24,000 of this was to purchase bread bags that would be sold later. The other significant expenditure was $12,000 for a portion of Mead's salary. Budget Printout, June 30, 1976, Abbey Archives, 318, Bread Budget.

34. Pillsbury paid royalties of $11,282 in fiscal year 1975. Since Holy Cross worked through Pillsbury, this included Saint John's share from that source. There are no separate records on how much Holy Cross contributed in fiscal year 1975, but $2,000 to $3,000 seems like a reasonable estimate. Budget Printout, June 30, 1976, Abbey Archives, 318, Bread Budget.

35. Materials for Royal Pantry Program, summer 1976, Abbey Archives, 318, Bread Frozen.

36. "Pedrizetti" is Father Ray Pedrizetti, OSB, a Duluth native on the faculty at Saint John's University. Tavis to Murphy, August 13, 1976, and attached, Abbey Archives, 320, Bread Correspondence.

37. It is clear that Star Markets of Cambridge, Massachusetts, and Acme Markets of Philadelphia, actually sold Johnnie Bread. The evidence also suggests that Eisner's of Indiana/Illinois, and the Strand Baking Company may have done so. See folders for each in Abbey Archives, 317.

38. Interview with Jerry Mead, September 12, 1996.

39. Interview with Father Gordon Tavis, August 9, 1994.

40. Mead to Ray, after November 25, 1975, Abbey Archives, 318, Bread Strategy/Policy/Legal.

41. Mead to Murray, November 13, 1975, Abbey Archives, 320, Bread Correspondence. The same month Saint John's stopped using Phillip Orth as a blender, even though Orth had been the most successful in soliciting new commercial clients. Mead to Ray, after November 25, 1975, Abbey Archives, 318, Bread Strategy/Policy/Legal.

42. Interview with Jerry Mead, September 12, 1996; Interview with Father Gordon Tavis, August 9, 1994.

43. Bread Sales, November 1974 and January 1975, Abbey Archives, Box 320, Income-Expenses.

44. In July, Mead asked Orth to provide five rail carloads of mix to five Southern cities by August. Mead to Ray, after November 25, 1975, Abbey Archives 318, Bread Strategy/Policy/Legal.

45. Mead was based in Alabama, and was paid a ten percent commission on mix sales in addition to his salary. Janzen to Mead, January 7, 1976, Abbey Archives, 318, Bread - Jerry Mead.

46. Interview with Jerry Mead, September 12, 1996; Presentation, Abbey Archives, 320, Slide Show.

47. Interview with Norm Groth, August 15, 1996.

48. Interview with Jerry Mead, September 12, 1996; Interview with Father Gordon Tavis, August 9, 1994. Interview with Carolyn Brown, July 17, 1996.

49. Interview with Jerry Mead, September 12, 1996.

50. Interview with Carolyn Brown, July 17, 1996.

51. Interview with Father Gordon Tavis, August 9, 1994.

52. Interview with Father Gordon Tavis, August 9, 1994.

53. Tavis to Hansen, October 7, 1975.

54. Rymer to Tavis, March 2, 1976, Abbey Archives, 318, Dogwood.

55. Hansen to Tavis, January 22, 1976.

56. Interview with Jerry Mead, September 12, 1996.

57. Rymer to Tavis, March 2, 1976, Abbey Archives, 318, Bread Budget.

58. Rymer to Tavis, May 7, 1976.

59. Mead to Tavis, May 13, 1976, Abbey Archives, 318, Dogwood.

60. Father Gordon had projected costs of $84,000, so the actual costs were about six percent over budget. Budget Printout, June 30, 1976, Abbey Archives, 318, Bread Budget.

61. In 1969, the net income was $12,176 on royalties of $13,318. In the year of Father Walter's death, the difference was only $327. Net income from "Saint John's Bread - Net Income," Saint John's Abbey Annual Reports, 1958-1973, Business Office. Royalty income from account statements from Russell-Miller/Peavey/Pillsbury, Abbey Archives. See also interview with Tom LeNeau, July 22, 1996.

62. The budget for fiscal year 1975 shows a transfer of $60,196, for "Deficit Old." Budget Printout, June 30, 1976, Abbey Archives, 318, Bread Budget.

63. Budget Printout, June 30, 1976, Abbey Archives, 318, Bread Budget.

64. Father Gordon's handwritten notes (no date), Abbey Archives, 318, Dogwood Pre-Contract.

65. Father Gordon's handwritten notes, "Kevin - with Austin, Jerry, Me" (no date), Abbey Archives, 318, Bread Strategy/Policy/Legal.

66. Father Gordon's handwritten notes.

67. Father Gordon's handwritten notes, "Kevin," October 7, 1975.

68. Father Gordon's handwritten notes.

69. Tavis to Executive Committee, October 7, 1976, Abbey Archives, 319, Dogwood Contract.

70. Interview with Father Gordon Tavis, August 9, 1994; Father Gordon's handwritten notes, "Kevin - with Austin, Jerry, and Me" (no date), Abbey Archives, 318, Bread Strategy/Policy/Legal.

71. Tavis to Regents' Finance Committee, October 19, 1976, Abbey Archives, 319, Dogwood Contract.

72. Father Gordon's handwritten notes, "Kevin - with Austin, Jerry, and Me" (no date), Abbey Archives, 318, Bread Strategy/Policy/Legal. For Father Gordon's concern with tax issues, see also Tavis to Richter, December 27, 1976, Abbey Archives, Bread Correspondence.

73. Tavis to Hansen, October 7, 1975, Abbey Archives, 318, Dogwood Pre-Contract.

74. Tavis to Executive Committee, October 7, 1976, Abbey Archives, 319, Dogwood Contract; Distribution and License Agreement, December 1976, Abbey Archives, 319, Contracts.

75. Points of Agreement, October 14, 1976, Abbey Archives, 319, Contracts; Distribution and License Agreements, December 1976, Abbey Archives, 319, Contracts.

76. Points of Agreement, October 14, 1976.

77. Points of Agreement, October 14, 1976.

78. Tavis to Richter, December 27, 1976.

79. The upper range was $75,000, depending on when Mead could be re-assigned. Tavis to Murray, February 4, 1977, Abbey Archives, 320, Bread Correspondence; Tavis to Regents' Finance Committee, October 19, 1976, Abbey Archives, 319, Dogwood Contract.

80. Contract, Abbey Archives, 319, Dogwood Contract.

81. Brokerage statements, Abbey Archives, 318, Griffith Sales Data.

82. Budget Printout, June 30, 1978, Abbey Archives, 318, Bread Budgets.

83. The deficit in fiscal year 1976 was $34,593. Budget Printouts, June 30, 1976 and June 30, 1978, Abbey Archives, 318, Bread Budget.

84. Budget Printout, June 30, 1978.

85. Danner to Tavis, May 16, 1978, Abbey Archives, 318, Griffith Communiques.

86. Tavis to Price, September 14, 1978, Abbey Archives, 318, Griffith Communiques.

87. Interview with Jerry Mead, September 12, 1996.

88. Interview with Father Gordon Tavis, August 9, 1994. Tom LeNeau suggests that the major companies were in the field all along, but expanded their efforts and Saint John's lacked the sales network to compete. Interview with Tom LeNeau, July 22, 1996.

89. Interview with Father Gordon Tavis, August 9, 1994.

90. Budget Printout, June 30, 1979.

91. Saint John's Abbey, fiscal year 1979, Abbey Archives, 320, Pillsbury Sales Data.

92. Interview with Father Gervase Soukup, July 7, 1995.

93. This figure does not count the $60,000 that was credited to the program in fiscal year 1975 to eliminate the "Deficit Old" that

apparently accumulated in the first part of the 1970s (Budget Printout, June 30, 1976, 318, Bread Budget). In 1977, financial officers at Saint John's were evidently still charging this debt against the bread program, for a memo asserted that the program owed the University Debt Service Reserve $94,134 for fiscal year 1975 and 1976 deficits at a time when the operating deficits for those years totaled approximately $34,000 (Janzen to Mead, March 11, 1977, 320, Bread Correspondence).

94. Tony Kennedy, "No Matter How You Slice It," Minneapolis *Star Tribune*, November 11, 1994, p. 1.

95. Interview with Rich Ruprecht, February 13, 1997.

96. Ruprecht says that discriminating monks can tell when he is on vacation because the slightly different mixing procedures used by other bakers change the texture. One key to the crust is that the Saint John's oven uses traditional dry heat, whereas most commercial bakeries add steam to create a softer crust. Interview with Rich Ruprecht, February 13, 1997.

97. Floor meetings sometimes order as many as 50 loaves. Interview with Rich Ruprecht, February 13, 1997; Dave McMahon, "Bread Dough, Baker, Munchy Maker," *Record*, October 5, 1982, p. 1.

98. Interview with Rich Ruprecht, February 13, 1997.

99. Author's correspondence with Food Service Director Dave Schoenberg, July 15, 1996. On a normal evening, Ruprecht makes 120-130 loaves of the dark bread. Interview with Rich Ruprecht, February 13, 1997.

100. Tony Kennedy, "No Matter How You Slice It," Minneapolis *Star Tribune*, October 11, 1994, p. 1.

About the Authors

Diane Veale Jones is an associate professor of Nutrition at the College of Saint Benedict/Saint John's University. She is a registered and licensed dietician who has written about ethnic foodways.

Kenneth M. Jones, whose specialty is recent United States history, is a professor of history at the College of Saint Benedict/Saint John's University.

This book began as a collaborative project between a dietician and an historian, but it evolved as the historical portian grew. Diane shaped the sections on the nature of bread and its nutritional properties, as well as providing criticism and support throughout. Ken did the archival research, interviews, and wrote the historical narrative.

Kenneth M. and Diane Veale Jones